Welcome to
Table Talk

Table Talk helps children and adults explore the Bible together. Each day provides a short family Bible time which, with your own adaptation, could work for ages 4 to 12. It includes optional follow–on material which takes the passage further for older children. There are also suggestions for linking **Table Talk** with **XTB** children's notes.

Who can use Table Talk?

Table Talk

A short family Bible time for daily use. Table Talk takes about five minutes, maybe at breakfast, or after an evening meal. Choose whatever time and place suits you best as a family. Table Talk includes a simple discussion starter or activity that leads into a short Bible reading. This is followed by a few questions.

- **Families**
- **One adult with one child**
- **A teenager with a younger brother or sister**
- **Children's leaders with their groups**
- **Any other mix that works for you!**

XTB

XTB children's notes help 7-11 year olds to get into the Bible for themselves. They are based on the same Bible passages as **Table Talk**. You will find suggestions for how **XTB** can be used alongside **Table Talk** on the next page.

In the next three pages you'll find suggestions for how to use Table Talk, along with hints and tips for adapting it to your own situation. If you've never done anything like this before, check out our web page for further help (go to www.thegoodbook.co.uk and click on Daily Reading) or write in for a fact sheet.

THE SMALL PRINT

Table Talk is published by The Good Book Company, 37 Elm Road, New Malden, Surrey, KT3 3HB
Tel: 0845 225 0880. www.thegoodbook.co.uk   email: alison@thegoodbook.co.uk   Written by Alison Mitchell.
Fab pictures by Kirsty McAllister. Bible quotations taken from the Good News Bible.
AUSTRALIA: Distributed by Matthias Media. Tel: (02) 9663 1478; email: info@matthiasmedia.com.au

HOW TO USE
Table Talk

Table Talk is designed to last for up to three months. How you use it depends on what works for you. We have included 65 full days of material in this issue, plus some more low-key suggestions for another 26 days (at the back of the book). We would like to encourage you to work at establishing a pattern of family reading. The first two weeks are the hardest!

DAY 1
What shall we do?

KEYPOINT
When the people heard Peter's speech, they asked, "What shall we do?" **Read Acts 2v38-39**

Today's passages are:
Table Talk : Acts 2v38-39
XTB : Acts 2v37-40

TABLE TALK **Recap:** Look again at yesterday's five points from Peter's speech.

READ When the people heard Peter's speech, they asked, "What shall we do?" **Read Acts 2v38-39**

TALK Peter told them to **repent**. What does that mean? (To repent doesn't just mean saying sorry. It means asking God to help you to **change**, and to do what He says.) What two things did Peter say would happen? (Their sins will be forgiven, they'll be given the gift of the Holy Spirit.)

DO Use the illustration in **Notes for Parents** (on the previous page) to show how Jesus rescues us from our sins.

PRAY Verse 39 means that this promise is for **us** too—even though we live 2000 years after Peter! Thank God for sending Jesus so that you can be forgiven.

Building up
The apostles had the task of telling others about Jesus. Some of them also wrote the books that make up the New T. But what if they **forgot** some of what they had seen or heard? Or didn't understand it? **Read John 14v25-26** to see how the Holy Spirit helped them. Thank God for making sure that what the apostles taught and wrote down about Jesus was true and accurate.

Table Talk is based on the same Bible passages as *XTB*, but usually only asks for two or three verses to be read out loud. The full *XTB* passage is listed at the top of each **Table Talk** page. If you are using **Table Talk** with older children, read the full *XTB* passage rather than the shorter version.

KEYPOINT
This is the main point you should be trying to convey. Don't read this out—it often gives away the end of the story!

The main part of **Table Talk** is designed to be suitable for younger children. *Building Up* includes more difficult questions designed for older children, or those with more Bible knowledge.

As far as possible, if your children are old enough to read the Bible verses for themselves, encourage them to find the answers in the passage and to tell you which verse the answer is in. This will help them to get used to handling the Bible for themselves.

The **Building Up** section is optional. It is designed to build on the passage studied in Table Talk (and XTB). Building Up includes some additional questions which reinforce the main teaching point, apply the teaching more directly, or follow up any difficult issues raised by the passage.

Linking with XTB

The **XTB** children's notes are based on the same passages as **Table Talk**. There are a number of ways in which you can link the two together:
- Children do **XTB** on their own. Parents then follow these up later (see suggestions below).
- A child and adult work through **XTB** together.
- A family uses **Table Talk** together at breakfast. Older children then use **XTB** on their own later.
- You use **Table Talk** on its own, with no link to **XTB**.

FOLLOWING UP XTB

If your child uses **XTB** on their own it can be helpful to ask them later to show you (or tell you) what they've done. Some useful starter questions are:

- Can you tell me what the reading was about?

- Is there anything you didn't understand or want to ask about?

- Did anything surprise you in the reading? Was there anything that would have surprised the people who first saw it or read about it?

- What did you learn about God, Jesus or the Holy Spirit?

- Is there anything you're going to do as a result of reading this passage?

Table Talk is deliberately not too ambitious. Most families find it quite hard to set up a regular pattern of reading the Bible together—and when they do meet, time is often short. So **Table Talk** is designed to be quick and easy to use, needing little in the way of extra materials, apart from pen and paper now and then.

BUT!!

Most families have special times when they **can** be more ambitious, or do have some extra time available. Here are some suggestions for how you can use **Table Talk** as the basis for a special family adventure...

PICNIC

Take Table Talk with you on a family picnic. Thank God for His beautiful Creation.

WALK

Go for a walk together. Stop somewhere with a good view and read Genesis 1v1—2v4.

GETTING TOGETHER

Invite another family for a meal, and to read the Bible together. The children could make a poster based on the passage.

MUSEUM

Visit a museum to see a display from Bible times. Use it to remind yourselves that the Bible tells us about real people and real history.

HOLIDAYS

Set aside a special time each day while on holiday. Choose some unusual places to read the Bible together—on the beach, up a mountain, in a boat... Take some photos to put on your Table Talk display when you get back from holiday.

You could try one of the special holiday editions of XTB and Table Talk—**Christmas Unpacked**, **Easter Unscrambled** and **Summer Signposts**.

Have an
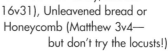
adventure!

FOOD!

Eat some food linked with the passage you are studying. For example Manna (biscuits made with honey, Exodus 16v31), Unleavened bread or Honeycomb (Matthew 3v4— but don't try the locusts!)

DISPLAY AREA

We find it easier to remember and understand what we learn when we have something to look at. Make a Table Talk display area, for pictures, Bible verses and prayers. Add to it regularly.

VIDEO

A wide range of Bible videos are available—from simple cartoon stories, to whole Gospels filmed with real life actors. (Your local Christian bookshop should have a range.) Choose one that ties in with the passages you are reading together. **_Note:_** Use the video **in addition** to the Bible passage, not **instead** of it!

PRAYER DIARY

As a special project, make a family prayer diary. Use it to keep a note of things you pray for—and the answers God gives you. This can be a tremendous help to children (and parents!) to learn to trust God in prayer as we see how He answers over time. Go on—try it!

DRAMA OR PUPPETS

Take time to dramatise a Bible story. Maybe act it out (with costumes if possible) or make some simple puppets to retell the story.

Enough of the introduction, let's get going...

HANDY HISTORY LESSON:

The book of **Daniel** fits in towards the end of Old Testament history. Use the Bible Timeline opposite, and the map below, to see how everything fits together:

- The Israelites used to live in <u>one</u> kingdom, called Israel. Their kings were Saul, David and Solomon.
- But then the kingdom was divided into <u>two</u>:
  —the biggest chunk was still called **Israel**.
  —the smaller bit was called **Judah**.
- God warned the people in **Israel** that if they <u>turned away</u> from Him, they would be <u>turned out</u> of their country.
  —but they didn't listen!

- So God allowed the **Assyrians** to capture Israel, and take the people away into exile (which means being sent away from your home and country).
- God also warned the people of **Judah** that the same thing would happen to <u>them</u> if they turned away from God
  —but they didn't listen either!
- So God allowed the **Babylonians** to zoom in and capture Judah, and take the people far away to Babylon.

Bible Timeline

The Bible Timeline opposite was designed for use with Issue 12 of XTB. If you would like a free copy of the Bible Timeline, please **write to:** Table Talk, The Good Book Company, 37 Elm Road, New Malden, Surrey, KT3 3HB **or email:** alison@thegoodbook.co.uk *Please mention that you are asking for a free copy to use with Table Talk.*

KEYPOINT
King Nebuchadnezzar <u>seemed</u> to be in charge—but **God** is the Real King!

Today's passages are:
Table Talk: Daniel 1v1-9
XTB: Daniel 1v1-9

TABLE TALK

<u>With older children</u>, read **Notes for Parents** together, and use the **Bible Timeline** (opposite <u>and</u> on Day 3) to see where Daniel fits in to Old Testament history. Then **read Daniel 1v1-9**.

READ

<u>With younger children</u>, don't read all the history in Notes for Parents. Just explain that God's people, the Israelites, had been captured by the Babylonians. God had allowed this because His people had turned away from Him. Ask them to find Daniel on the Bible Timeline (opposite and on Day 3), then **read Daniel 1v1-9**.

TALK

King Nebuchadnezzar wanted some of the young men from Judah to be trained to serve him. But King Neb was very fussy! What were they to be like? (v3-4) (*Young, healthy, good looking, quick at learning, from royal or noble families.*) How long were they to be trained for? (v5) (*Three years*)

THINK

King Neb was rich and powerful, and ruled over the huge Babylonian empire. He <u>seemed</u> to be the most powerful king around... **BUT who** gave Judah and its king into King Neb's hands? (v2) (<u>God</u> *did*.) And who made the Babylonian official kind to Daniel? (v9) (<u>God did</u>.)

HISTORY = H_____ S_____
(*The answer's on the Bible Timeline.*)

PRAY

Thank God that <u>He</u> is the **Real King** of everyone and everything. Ask Him to help you learn more about Him as you read the book of Daniel together.

Building up
Check out the rest of the **Bible Timeline** together.

DAY 2 The best of the bunch

KEYPOINT
God gave Daniel and co. their abilities. <u>Our</u> abilities come from God too.

Today's passages are:
Table Talk: Daniel 1v11-21
XTB: Daniel 1v8-21

TABLE TALK

Put a variety of different foods on the table (include water and some vegetables). Ask your child which they would choose to eat and drink, and why.

Daniel and his three friends were being trained to serve King Nebuchadnezzar. They were supposed to eat the food and wine from the king's table—but Daniel refused! We don't know exactly what was wrong with the royal food and wine. But Daniel thought he'd be offending God if he ate it. So he refused to eat it!

READ

The Babylonians could have been very angry. But as we saw yesterday, <u>God</u> made the Babylonian official kind to Daniel. So Daniel suggested a kind of test... **Read Daniel 1v11-21**

TALK

What did Daniel and his friends eat and drink? (v12) (*Vegetables and water.*) Did they stay healthy? (v15) (*Very!*) What did God give Daniel? (v17) (*Knowledge and the ability to understand dreams.*)

At the end of the three years, King Neb tested everyone who had been trained, and chose the best of the bunch to serve him. Who did he choose? (v19) (*Daniel and his friends.*)

PRAY

King Neb chose the best of the bunch, but it was **God** who gave them their abilities! What are <u>you</u> good at? Thank God for the abilities He has given you. Ask Him to help you use them to serve Him.

Building up

What kind of things might others expect us to do, that don't honour God? (*eg: joining in with gossip.*) Ask God to help you live in a way that honours Him.

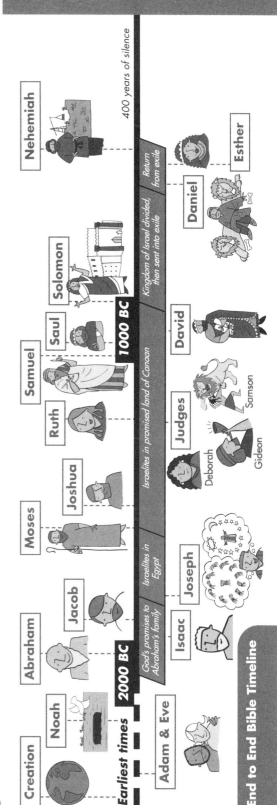

JESUS 6 BC—30 AD

Nehemiah

400 years of silence

Esther

Return from exile

Daniel

Kingdom of Israel divided, then sent into exile

Solomon

Saul

David

1000 BC

Samuel

Israelites in promised land of Canaan

Judges

Samson

Ruth

Deborah

Gideon

Joshua

Moses

Joseph

Jacob

Israelites in Egypt

Abraham

God's promises to Abraham's family

Isaac

2000 BC

Earliest times

Creation

Noah

Adam & Eve

End to End Bible Timeline

JESUS — 6 BC–30 AD

The Church begins

Peter

Paul

John's vision of heaven

HISTORY = HIS STORY

The Bible is <u>God's</u> Word to us. It tells us **His** story, starting with the creation of the world and going on for ever and ever!

The people in this timeline all knew that God is the <u>Real King</u> of everyone and everything. Christians today believe that too—and look forward to living with God for ever in heaven.

Life of Jesus

Birth

Baptism — This is my Son

Miracles

Teaching

Death and Resurrection

Ascension

1000 AD

2000 AD

Christians today

Jesus comes back. End of the world.

The future

A new heaven and a new earth

DAY 3
Bad dreams

🔑 **KEYPOINT**
When he was in trouble, Daniel prayed. So can we.

Today's passages are:
Table Talk: Daniel 2v1-4 & 14-18
XTB: Daniel 2v1-18

TABLE TALK
Talk about any strange or funny dreams you've had recently.

READ
King Neb had a bad dream. He had no idea what it meant. But he had lots of advisers whose job was to answer difficult questions—so he called them in to explain the dream... **Read Daniel 2v1-4**

TALK
When King Neb asked what his dream meant, how did his advisers reply? (v4) (*'Tell us your dream and we will explain it.'*) But it wasn't going to be that easy! King Neb <u>refused</u> to tell them his dream.

> Tell me the dream. Then I will know that you can also tell me what it means.

But they couldn't do it! Nobody knew what the king had dreamt.

King Neb was furious! He ordered that all of his advisers must be **killed**—including Daniel and his friends! **Read Daniel 2v14-18**

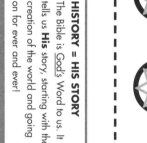

TALK
What did Daniel ask the king for? (v16) (*For time, so that he could explain the dream.*) What did Daniel tell his friends to do? (v18) (*Pray to God for help.*) How do you think God answered their prayers? *We'll find out tomorrow...*

PRAY
If you find yourself in a tricky situation... PRAY! Get your friends to pray for you too. Pray together now about anything you are worried about.

Building up
Read the middle of the story in **Daniel 2v5-13**. Verse 11 says that 'the gods do not live among men'. Which God <u>did</u> live with His people on earth? (*Jesus*)

DAY 4
Visions and dreams

TABLE TALK

(*You need pencil and paper.*) Make a list of words that describe what God is like. Keep your list for later.

READ

King Neb was angry! Nobody could tell him his dream. So he ordered that all of his advisers must be killed! But Daniel and his friends knew that **God** is the **Real King** of everyone and everything. So they prayed to God for help...
Read Daniel 2v19

THINK

Wow! Daniel had a dream too—in which God showed him everything he needed to know to help King Neb. How do you think Daniel <u>felt</u>?

READ

Daniel thanked and praised God...
Read Daniel 2v20-23

How long is God to be praised? (v20) (*For ever and ever.*) What does God control? (v21) (*Times and seasons; kings.*) What does God give? (v21-23) (*Wisdom and knowledge.*)

THINK

Did any of the things in Daniel's prayer match the list you made earlier? Do you want to add anything to your list, now that you've read Daniel's prayer?

PRAY

Now use your list to thank and praise God for who He is and what He has done for you.

Building up
Read v22 again. The reason we can know God is because <u>He</u> has revealed Himself to us. How can we know what God is like? (*By reading His Word to us, the Bible. And by looking at Jesus—John 14v8-10.*)

DAY 5
Smashing statue

TABLE TALK

<u>Recap:</u> King Neb had a bad dream. What did he want his advisers to do? (*Tell him the dream, and what it meant.*) Could they do it? (*No!*) King Neb was furious! What did he decide to do? (*Have all of his advisers killed.*) But Daniel prayed for help. What did God do? (*Told Daniel all about King Neb's dream.*)

DO

Daniel went to see King Neb. *Find out what happened by reading the **cartoon story** over the page.*
Then read Daniel 2v36-45

TALK

King Neb's dream was about the **future**. King Neb was the head of gold. He and his kingdom (the Babylonians) were strong and powerful. But <u>who</u> gave them that power? (v37) (*God*)

After the Babylonians would come several more kingdoms. Each would be less powerful than the one before. The last kingdom would be divided.

THINK

The **rock** in the dream stands for a kingdom that will last for ever. Who set this kingdom up? (v44) (*The God of heaven.*) The rock was the start of this great kingdom. The rock was actually a <u>person</u> who God sent to be King. Check out the big solid block on your **Bible Timeline** to see <u>who</u> it was. (*Jesus*)

PRAY

Jesus is the King of the universe. His kingdom will rule for ever! If you're a Christian (a follower of Jesus) then you're a part of that amazing kingdom! How does that make you feel? Talk to God about it now.

DAY 5
Notes for Parents

No <u>man</u> can tell you what you dreamt.

But there is a <u>God</u> in heaven who reveals mysteries.

You saw an enormous dazzling statue.

The head of the statue was made of pure gold.

Its chest and arms were of silver.

Its legs were of iron.

Its middle and thighs were of bronze.

And its feet partly of iron and partly of clay.

Then you saw a rock, which hit the statue.

The statue was broken into pieces and blew away

But the rock became a huge mountain and filled the whole earth.

Taken from Daniel 2v24-35.

DAY 6
How high???

KEYPOINT
S,M&A were determined to put God first.

Today's passages are:
Table Talk: Daniel 3v1 & 13-18
XTB: Daniel 3v1-18

TABLE TALK

God had helped Daniel to explain the king's dream to him. As a result, King Neb learnt something very important about God: **read Daniel 2v47**

READ

It looks like King Neb had got his thinking right at last. He knew that **God** is the <u>Real King</u>. But then he did something very wrong... **Read Daniel 3v1**

TALK

King Neb built a HUGE gold statue. How high was it? (v1) (90 ft/27 m)

King Neb gathered all the most important people in the country and forced them to bow down and worship the statue. Anyone who refused would be thrown into a blazing furnace!

READ

Daniel and his friends knew that **God** is the <u>Real King</u>. It would be very wrong to worship anyone or anything else. Daniel's friends S,M&A (Shadrach, Meshach and Abednego) were in the crowd in front of the statue. But they <u>refused</u> to bow down to it! **Read Daniel 3v13-18**

TALK

What did S,M&A say to King Neb? (v17-18) ('The God we serve is able to save us. But even if He does not, we will not serve your gods or worship the gold statue you have set up.')

PRAY

S,M&A knew that God could save them from the flames. But even if He didn't, they were determined to put God first, and not bow down to a statue! Do <u>you</u> want to put God first in your life? Then ask Him to help you, even when it's hard.

Building up
Talk about any times when obeying God has been hard, but turned out to be the best.

DAY 7
Facing the fire

KEYPOINT
A man appeared in the furnace with S,M&A. All four were walking about, unharmed.

Today's passages are:
Table Talk: Daniel 3v19-27
XTB: Daniel 3v19-27

TABLE TALK

Quick Quiz: 1—What did King Neb build? (*A huge gold statue.*) **2**—What did he order the people to do? (*Worship the gold statue.*) **3**—What would happen if anyone disobeyed? (*They'd be thrown into a blazing furnace!*) **4**—Who refused to worship the statue? (*S,M&A*) **5**—Why wouldn't S,M&A bow to a statue? (*Because God is the Real King.*)

READ

King Neb was furious with S,M&A. He ordered the furnace to be made seven times hotter than usual. Then S,M&A were tied up and thrown in!!! **Read Daniel 3v19-27**

TALK

King Neb expected to see three men in the furnace, tied up and dying. What did he actually see? (v24-25) (*Four men, untied, walking around unharmed.*)

Wow! A man appeared in the furnace with S,M&A. All four were walking around in the fire—untied and unharmed!

God doesn't always save Christians like this. BUT He sent Jesus to rescue <u>all</u> Christians from <u>the worst</u> danger ever. (*More about this on Day 30.*)

THINK

God <u>does</u> allow hard things to happen (often to teach us something) but He is always **with us**, and will **help us** when we ask. Is anything bad or sad worrying you? Talk to God about it, and ask Him to help you. He will!

Building up
Why does God allow hard things to happen to us? Part of the answer is in **Hebrews 12v7-11**. (*God allows it for our good, to make us more like Jesus.*)

DAY 8
The God who rescues

KEYPOINT
God is the God who **rescues**. He rescued S,M&A. And He sent Jesus to be our Rescuer.

Today's passages are:
Table Talk: Daniel 3v28-30
XTB: Daniel 3v28-30

TABLE TALK

(*You'll need your* **Bible Timeline** *[opposite Day 1] for today's Table Talk.*)

READ

1—**About 600BC**
(Daniel on Timeline)
King Neb had been <u>sure</u> that his furnace would kill S,M&A. Before he threw them in, he said, "What God will be able to rescue you from my hand?". (3v15) But now he knew that everything S,M&A had told him about God was true... **Read Daniel 3v28-30**

TALK

Why did King Neb praise God? (v28) (*Because God sent His angel to rescue S,M&A.*) What had King Neb learnt about God? (v29) (*No other god can save in this way.*)

THINK

King Neb was right that only **God** could rescue His people like this. But God was going to do an even more amazing rescue...

2—**About 30AD** (Solid block on Timeline) Who lived, died and came back to life again as our Rescuer? (*Jesus*) *We'll find out more about how Jesus rescues us on Day 21.*

PRAY

3—**Today** (After 2000AD on Timeline) Christians are people who have been rescued by Jesus and follow Him as their King. They look forward to living with Jesus in heaven. If that includes you, thank God for sending Jesus as your Rescuer. If you're not sure, ask God to help you find out more as you read the Bible together.

Building up
See how Jesus describes His rescue mission in **Luke19v10**.

DAY 9
Stumped by a dream

Today's passages are:
Table Talk: Daniel 4v9-18
XTB: Daniel 4v1-18

(*You each need pencil and paper.*) Each draw a tall tree. Add some fruit growing on it. Then draw birds in the tree and animals sheltering under it.

The next chapter of Daniel was written by King Neb himself! He tells us about a dream he had, of a tree like the one you've just drawn. No one could explain the dream, so he turned to Daniel (who he called Belteshazzar). **Read Daniel 4v9-18**

TALK

The tree was large and strong—but what did an angel say would happen to it? (v14) (*It must be cut down.*) What would be left? (v15) (*The stump and roots, with a band of iron and bronze.*)

THINK

The tree in the dream was a picture of a person. He would be cut down from his powerful position and become like an animal! He would live outside among the plants until seven years had passed. Verse 17 gives the reason for this. What will it show people about God (the Most High)? (v17) (*He is sovereign over human kingdoms, and gives them to whoever He chooses.*)

PRAY

God is the **Real King** (sovereign). That means God is in control of everything. He has the power to do anything at all! Do you know God is in charge of _your_ life too? Talk to Him about how you can live for Him.

Building up
As I write this, there's a General Election in Great Britain. What do these verses say about governments and politicians? Talk about how you might pray for them—then do it!

DAY 10
Pride and prejudice

Today's passages are:
Table Talk: Daniel 4v28-33
XTB: Daniel 4v19-33

TABLE TALK

Recap: What did King Neb see in his dream? (*A huge, strong tree.*) What happened to it? (*It was cut down.*) What was left? (*A stump.*)

Daniel warned King Neb that he was the powerful tree that would be cut down. But King Neb was too **proud** to do anything about it. Instead, he boasted about his own power and glory! **Read Daniel 4v28-33**

TALK

When did all this happen to King Neb? (v29) (*A year after his dream.*) What did he boast about? (v30) (*How great Babylon was, and how it displayed his power and glory.*) Everything then happened exactly as God had said. King Neb was kicked out of Babylon and lived like a wild animal, eating grass. He even started to look like an animal!

King Neb was too proud. He ignored all the things he'd learnt about God. He still thought he was more important than anyone—even God! Pride is wrong, because **God** is the greatest and **He's** the One in control of everything.

THINK

PRAY

Tell God about any times you've been proud. Say sorry and ask Him to help you change.

Building up
Check out the things King Neb knew about God in **Daniel 2v37**, **2v47** and **3v28**.

DAY 11
King of kings

KEYPOINT
When God gave King Neb his mind back, he praised God as the King of Kings.

Today's passages are:
Table Talk: Daniel 4v1-3 & 34-37
XTB: Daniel 4v1-3 & 34-37

TABLE TALK

Imagine that something amazing happens to you (eg: you're invited to star in a TV show, or meet your favourite sports star...) If you then wrote a <u>letter</u> to tell someone about it, **who** would you write to?

Chapter 4 of Daniel is a **letter** written by Kind Neb. Today we'll read the <u>end</u> of it...

READ

King Neb lived like an animal for seven years. He even ate grass! Then God gave him his mind back—and he praised God as the King of Kings...
Read Daniel 4v34-37

TALK

What had King Neb learnt about God?
• About God's rule (dominion) and kingdom (v34)? (*They last for all time.*)
• What does God do? (v35) (*No one can stop Him! He does whatever He wants.*)
• Is God right or wrong? (v37) (*Everything He does is right and just [fair].*)

READ

Neb became king again—just as God said he would. In fact, he was even more powerful than he was before! But this time, King Neb used his power to tell other people about God. **Read Daniel 4v1-3**

Who did King Neb tell about God? (v1) (*Everyone!*)

PRAY

If you're a Christian, then God has done an amazing miracle in <u>your</u> life. He has rescued you! Think again about the people you would have written to about being on TV etc. Can you be like King Neb and write to one of them about God??? Ask God to help you do that today.

Building up
Copy **Daniel 4v3** onto some paper. Display it where you will all see it.

DAY 12
Write and wrong

KEYPOINT
Belshazzar used cups from God's temple to praise pretend gods.

Today's passages are:
Table Talk: Daniel 5v1-9
XTB: Daniel 5v1-9

TABLE TALK

The book of Daniel now jumps ahead a few years. King Neb is dead and King Belshazzar is in charge of Babylonia.
Read Daniel 5v1-4

Belshazzar had a huge party. What did they drink from? (v2) (*The goblets that had been taken from God's temple in Jerusalem.*) These goblets had been made to praise the One True God. But who did Belshazzar praise with them? (v4) (*Pretend gods made of gold, wood etc.*)

TALK

DO

Suddenly, something frightening appeared on the wall! *Join the dots to see what it was.*

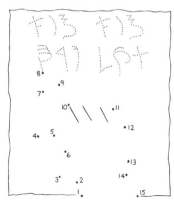

Belshazzar was terrified! **Read Dan 5v5-9**

How many of the king's advisers could help him? (v8) (*None*) But there was one man who <u>could</u> read the writing on the wall. *Tomorrow, **Daniel** will tell Belshazzar (and us!) what it said...*

TALK

I'm sure you've never done what Belshazzar did! But have you ever disrespected God? (*Told wrong jokes? Made fun of the Bible? Messed around when someone is teaching you the Bible?*) If you have, say sorry to God. Ask Him to help you show Him respect.

PRAY

Building up
Read the history of these goblets going to Babylon in **2 Kings 20v16-18** and **2 Kings 24v10-16**.

DAY 13
Read it write

Today's passages are:
Table Talk: Daniel 5v22-31
XTB: Daniel 5v10-31

TABLE TALK

Recap: What did King Belshazzar drink wine from? (*The goblets from God's temple.*) What suddenly appeared? (*A hand, writing on the wall.*) How did Belshazzar feel? (*Terrified—his knees were knocking! v6*)

READ

None of the king's advisers could read the writing. But then **Daniel** was brought in. Daniel reminded Belshazzar of everything that had happened to King Neb. Belshazzar <u>knew</u> these things, but he still hadn't cared about God...
Read Daniel 5v22-28

TALK

Who did Belshazzar praise? (v23) (*Pretend gods which cannot see, hear or understand.*) Who <u>didn't</u> he honour? (v23) (*The One True God who has power over his life and all he does.*)

THINK

The mysterious hand wrote these words: ***MENE, MENE, TEKEL, PARSIN***. They mean *number, number, weight, division*. Belshazzar's days were **numbered**. When **weighed** and measured against God's perfect standards, Belshazzar had completely failed. His kingdom was going to be **divided**. It would be taken over by the Medes and Persians.

READ

God's message to Belshazzar came true that night! **Read Daniel 5v29-31**

PRAY

The One True God has power over <u>your</u> life too! How does that make you feel? Talk to Him about it.

Building up
Read what the book of Proverbs says about pride: **Proverbs 11v2, 16v18, 29v23**.

DAY 14
Daniel's habit

Today's passages are:
Table Talk: Daniel 6v1-10
XTB: Daniel 6v1-10

TABLE TALK

Talk about any habits you have. (*Good habits as well as bad ones!*)

Daniel had a habit: **Daniel prayed**. Sounds like a great habit. But in today's story, some wicked men use Daniel's habit to get him into trouble! **Read Daniel 6v1-5**

READ

TALK

The new king, Darius, found that Daniel was hard-working and good at his job. So Darius wanted to put Daniel in charge of everything. The other officials tried to get Daniel into trouble. But what was their problem? (v4) (*Daniel had done nothing wrong.*)

THINK

Wow! By this time Daniel was over 80 years old. But his enemies couldn't find anything that he'd done wrong! Do you think that would be true of <u>your</u> life?

READ

Daniel's enemies set a trap for him. First, they persuaded King Darius to make a new law... **Read Daniel 6v6-10**

TALK

What a terrible law! For a whole month, no one was allowed to pray to anyone except the king. If they did, what would happen to them? (v7) (*They'd be thrown to the lions.*) But what did Daniel do when he heard about the new law? (v10) (*Daniel prayed.*) It looks like Daniel's going to be in a lot of trouble! *We'll find out tomorrow...*

PRAY

Do you want to have a praying habit like Daniel's? Talk about how you might do that—then ask God to help you.

Building up
Read Jesus' teaching about prayer in **Luke 11v1-10**.

DAY 15
Roaring rescue

TABLE TALK

What was Daniel's habit? (*He prayed.*)

Daniel's enemies had tricked King Darius into making a law that said no one was allowed to pray to anyone except the king. Now they were ready to trap Daniel...
READ
Read Daniel 6v11-16

King Darius desperately wanted to save Daniel—but even the <u>king</u> wasn't allowed to break the new law! What did he say to Daniel? (v16) (*'May your God, whom you serve continually, rescue you.'*)

READ
Darius <u>couldn't</u> save Daniel—but he hoped that God (the Real King!) <u>could</u>.
Read Daniel 6v17-23

TALK
Find <u>three</u> reasons why the lions didn't eat Daniel (v22-23) (*God's angel shut the lions mouths; Daniel was innocent in God's sight; Daniel had trusted God.*) God had kept Daniel totally safe. He wasn't even scratched!

THINK
Daniel chose to keep praying to God. As a result, he got into trouble and was thrown to the lions. The same will sometimes be true for us. We will get hassle for being Christians. God won't always stop us from having trouble. But we can be sure that He will be with us and help us.

PRAY
Thank God that He's always with His people. Ask Him to help you to trust Him as Daniel did.

Building up
Who <u>couldn't</u> save Daniel? (Daniel 6v14) (*King Darius.*) Why not? (v15) (*He wasn't allowed to break his own laws!*) Who <u>could</u> save Daniel? (*God*) Why? (*God is the Real King—see Daniel 4v34-35.*)

DAY 16
The living God

TABLE TALK
Play a game of **Hangman** to guess the phrase 'The living God who rescues.'

King Darius was thrilled that God had saved Daniel from the lions. He wrote a letter to all the people in his empire, telling them about the living God who rescues. Look out for these words as you read the king's letter
READ
for yourselves. **Read Daniel 6v25-28**

DO
Make a list of the things Darius had learnt about God.

PRAY
God never changes, so all of these things are true today as well. Use your list to thank and praise God for who He is and what He has done for you.

Building up
Darius wrote a letter <u>about</u> God. How about writing a letter <u>to</u> God—telling Him how you feel about Him and thanking Him for what He's done for you? Keep your letter in your Bible to remind you of the things you've learnt about God.

DAY 17
Daniel's dream

KEYPOINT
Daniel's dream is difficult—but it's very clear that **God** is in charge. He's the King of Kings.

Today's passages are:
Table Talk: Daniel 7v1-10
XTB: Daniel 7v1-10

TABLE TALK

Daniel 7 is a flashback, to the time when Belshazzar was king. In this chapter, Daniel tells us about a very odd dream in which he sees four strange beasts...
Read Daniel 7v1-8

DO

Write the correct verse number by each pic:

v____   v____

v____   v____

READ

Later on, we're told that the four beasts stand for four different kingdoms (v17). (*Like Babylonia, Persia, Greece and the Roman Empire, who were all powerful at different times.*) But these powerful kingdoms only seem to be in charge. In the next part of Daniel's dream, he sees the Real King... **Read Daniel 7v9-10**

THINK

Daniel saw **God** on the throne. He's the Real King. He is called the 'Ancient of Days' (your Bible may say 'One who has been living for ever'). God has always existed and always will. He rules for ever!

PRAY

Daniel's dream is hard to understand. But one thing that's very clear is that **God** is in charge. He is the King of Kings and will rule for ever. Thank Him for this.

Building up
Read v9 again. What did God look like? (*His clothes and hair were white.*) White is pure. God is pure and perfect. Everything He does is good and right. What was His throne like? (*Flaming with fire.*) God is also powerful, and will punish those who go against Him. He is in total control.

DAY 18
The Son of Man

KEYPOINT
Daniel had a vision of Jesus, the Son of Man. God made Jesus the ruler of everything.

Today's passages are:
Table Talk: Daniel 7v13-14
XTB: Daniel 7v11-14

TABLE TALK

Make a list of powerful people who are in charge of others (*eg: Prime Minister, American President, school headteacher, your boss at work...*)

READ

Daniel is having a strange dream, with weird beasts that stand for different kingdoms, and God sitting on a throne of fire. Then Daniel saw someone very special... **Read Daniel 7v13-14**

THINK

Daniel saw someone 'like a son of man' (v13). Some Bibles translate this as 'like a human being', but that means you might miss an exciting link with the New Testament, because 'Son of Man' is the name <u>Jesus</u> called Himself (*eg: John 9v35-37, Mark 2v10-12 and Matthew 12v40.*) The person Daniel saw in his dream was **Jesus**!

TALK

What was Jesus given? (v14) (*Authority, glory and power.*) What did the people of all nations do? (v14) (*Worshipped Jesus.*) What does v14 tell us about Jesus' kingdom? (*It will never be destroyed.*)

THINK

Jesus wasn't just the tiny baby we remember at Christmas. He is the powerful, conquering King. He is <u>far</u> more powerful than the people you listed! He will destroy all His enemies and one day, everyone will worship Him.

PRAY

Tell Jesus how great He is. Ask Him to be King of every part of your lives.

Building up
There's also a little horn in Daniel's dream. A horn was a picture of great power—but this horn still had far <u>less</u> power than God! **Read Daniel 7v11-12**. This horn was a picture of a proud king who spoke against God and made God's people suffer (v25). But **no one** is more powerful than God—so this proud king was defeated.

DAY 19
Daniel prays

Today's passages are:
Table Talk: Daniel 9v1-4, 9 & 19
XTB: Daniel 9v1-19

TABLE TALK

Do you remember what Daniel's habit was? (*He prayed.*) Today we get to listen in as Daniel reads the Bible and prays.
Read Daniel 9v1-3

TALK

What Old Testament book was Daniel reading? (v2) (*Jeremiah.*) How long did he read that Jerusalem would be in ruins for? (v2) (*70 years*) What did Daniel do? (v3) (*Prayed, fasted and wore sackcloth and ashes, to show his sadness.*)

DO

*Check out your **Bible Timeline***. God's people were in <u>exile</u> (sent away from Israel and Jerusalem). This was their punishment for turning away from God. But God had promised to bring His people back home after 70 years. This is the promise Daniel read in Jeremiah 29v10.

READ

Daniel's prayer is l-o-n-g, with some tricky words, so we're going to dip into three verses that sum it up.

• **God keeps His c_____**
(Daniel 9v4). God <u>always</u> keeps His promises (covenants). So Daniel prayed that God would keep His promise to end the exile after 70 years.

• **God is m_____ and f_____**
(Daniel 9v9) God's people had turned away from Him. But Daniel prayed that God would forgive them.

• **God's N_____ matters**
(Dan 9v19) It mattered to Daniel that God got the respect and glory He deserved.

PRAY

Turn these three things into prayer.

Building up
Check out God's promise in Jeremiah 29v10.

DAY 20
God's flying answer

Today's passages are:
Table Talk: Daniel 9v20-23 & 25
XTB: Daniel 9v20-27

TABLE TALK

What promise had Daniel been asking God to keep? (*To bring His people back home to Jerusalem.*) Straight away God sent an angel to give Daniel the answer!
Read Daniel 9v20-23

What was the angel called? (v21) (*Gabriel*) How quickly did God answer Daniel's prayer? (v23) (*As soon as Daniel began to pray.*)

THINK

When you write a letter, you sometimes wait ages for a reply. But when you pray, God hears you straight away—and He's never slow at answering! Sometimes His answer will be 'No' or 'Wait'—but God always answers our prayers.

READ

Like Daniel's prayer, Gabriel's answer is tricky to understand. So we'll just look at the clear and important things in one verse: **read Daniel 9v25**

DO

• Just as God promised, His people would return to Israel and rebuild Jerusalem. *Check out your **Bible Timeline** to see when this happened. This is the pic to look for.*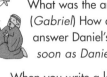

• After Jerusalem was rebuilt, God's chosen King (Anointed One) would come. That's Jesus. *Find the birth of Jesus on your **Bible Timeline**.*

PRAY

Jesus is going to come back to earth again. The world will end, and all of God's people will live with King Jesus in heaven. <u>Daniel</u> will be there! If you're a follower of Jesus, so will <u>you</u>! Talk to Him about this now.

Building up
Read another message from Gabriel in **Luke 1v26-33**.

WELCOME TO JOHN'S GOSPEL!

'Gospel' is a Greek word that means 'Good News'. John's book tells us the **good news** about **Jesus**.

At the end of his book—in John 20v31—John tells us <u>why</u> he wrote it:

> So that you may believe that Jesus is the Christ, the Son of God, and that by believing you may have life in His name.

John wants us to believe that Jesus is the **Christ** (Messiah). That means **God's chosen King**.

In his book, John tells us loads of amazing things that Jesus did and said. They are all **signposts** pointing to <u>who</u> Jesus is. They help us understand more about Jesus.

Many of these signposts pointed to something amazing about Jesus—He came to earth so that He could **die** for us!

KEYPOINT
Jesus let Himself be arrested because He knew He had to die.

Today's passages are:
Table Talk: John 18v1-11
XTB: John 18v1-11

TABLE TALK In the last few issues of Table Talk we've been reading John's book about Jesus. Read **Notes for Parents** together to check out what John's book is about.

READ The end of John's book tells us about the very first Easter. It started in a quiet garden... **Read John 18v1-6**

TALK Who came to find Jesus in the garden? (v2) (*Judas*) Judas was one of Jesus' disciples, His closest friends. Yet Judas handed Jesus over to be arrested by His enemies. What a traitor!

THINK What does v4 tell us about Jesus? (*He knew everything that was going to happen to Him.*) Jesus <u>knew</u> that He would be arrested and would be killed. Jesus was surrounded by soldiers yet **He** was in control! What did the soldiers do when they heard who He was? (v6) (*They fell to the ground.*)

READ **Read John 18v7-11**

TALK Jesus is so loving! Even when He was being arrested, He put others first. What did He make sure of? (v8) (*That His disciples could get away.*) And He didn't want Peter to cut off the guard's ear. Luke 22v51 says that Jesus healed the guard!

PRAY Jesus let Himself be arrested because He knew He had to die. It was all part of God's amazing plan to rescue people. Say **thank you** to Jesus for giving up His life for people like you and me.

Building up
Check out some other parts of John's book that show us that Jesus had to die. **Read John 2v18-22; 7v33-34; 12v1-8; 12v32-33**.

DAY 22
Don't keep quiet

KEYPOINT
Peter refused to admit that he knew Jesus. We should be ready to tell others we love Jesus.

Today's passages are:
Table Talk: John 18v15-18
XTB: John 18v12-18

TABLE TALK

Do people at school or work ever ask you (or tease you) about being a Christian? How do you answer? Are you honest or do you keep quiet?

READ

Jesus had been arrested and taken to the Jewish high priest. Peter followed Jesus to find out what would happen to Him. **Read John 18v15-18**

TALK

The 'other disciple' with Peter was probably John. He knew the high priest, and was able to get Peter into the courtyard. But then the girl at the gate recognised Peter! What did she say to him? (*See v17*) How did Peter answer? (v17) (*'I am not!'*)

Yesterday, we read how Peter <u>fought</u> for Jesus. Now he won't even say that he <u>knows</u> Jesus!

DO

Peter had to learn a hard lesson. But later, he changed and wrote **1 Peter 3v15**. Look it up to see what Peter had learnt.

PRAY

That means Christians should be ready to tell people about Jesus. Ask God to give you the courage to let your friends know that you love Jesus.

Building up
Read John 18v12-14. Jesus was taken to Caiaphas, the very important Jewish high priest. He hated Jesus so much that he wanted to kill Him. In a few day's time we'll see if Caiaphas got his wish.

DAY 23
Trial and error

KEYPOINT
Jesus was put on trial—but there was no proof against Him, no witnesses, and no fairness.

Today's passages are:
Table Talk: John 18v19-24
XTB: John 18v19-24

DO

Play **hangman** to guess these three words: *Proof, Witnesses, Fairness*.
(*To save time, do all three together.*)

READ

After His arrest, Jesus was put on trial. That means He was questioned by the Jewish leaders. But as we'll see, there was no proof, no witnesses, and no fairness! **Read John 18v19-24**

TALK

What did the high priest question Jesus about? (v19) (*His disciples and His teaching.*)

BUT there was no **proof** against Jesus (v20). He had done <u>nothing</u> wrong! He taught openly in the synagogue where people met to learn about God. He wasn't doing bad things secretly.

What did Jesus say the high priest should do? (v21) (*Question people who had heard Him.*) Loads of people could have spoken up for Jesus but were not given the chance. These **witnesses** would have told the priests the truth about Jesus.

What did the guard do to Jesus? (v22) (*He hit Jesus in the face.*) They had no proof against Jesus, but wouldn't let Him go. Instead, they sent Him to Caiaphas for another **unfair** trial.

PRAY

Jesus wasn't going to die for His <u>own</u> wrong—He hadn't done any wrong! Instead He would die for <u>our</u> wrong. Thank Him for this now.

Building up
Look back through John's Gospel at some of the headings. What kinds of things could witnesses have told the priests about what Jesus did and said?

DAY 24
Chicken!

KEYPOINT
Jesus had said that Peter would deny knowing Him three times. Jesus was right.

Today's passages are:
Table Talk: John 18v25-27
XTB: John 18v25-27

TABLE TALK

Flashback: Jesus had been arrested and Peter had followed Him. Let's find out what Jesus said to Peter earlier that evening... **Read John 13v36-38**

TALK

What did Peter say he was ready to do? (v37) (*To die for Jesus.*) But what did Jesus say Peter would do? (v38) (*Deny knowing Jesus.*) When would Peter say he didn't know Jesus? (v38) (*Before the cock crowed.*)

READ

Two days ago we read about Peter telling a girl that he didn't know Jesus. What do you think will happen next...?
Read John 18v25-27

TALK

Jesus was right. Peter denied knowing Jesus three times. And then what happened? (v27) (*A cock crowed.*)

How do you think Peter felt when he realised what he had done?

THINK

We all let Jesus down sometimes. Have you ever kept quiet while people made fun of Jesus? Or said that you did 'not much' on Sunday instead of mentioning church? Or felt too embarrassed to tell your friends that you love Jesus?

PRAY

Say sorry to God for the times you have let Him down.
Ask Him to help you be braver so you talk to your friends about Jesus.

Building up
Read Luke's account of this same story in **Luke 22v54-62**.

DAY 25
Pilate plot

KEYPOINT
The Jewish leaders were plotting to have Jesus killed, but it was His plan that was working out!

Today's passages are:
Table Talk: John 18v28-32
XTB: John 18v28-32

TABLE TALK

Yesterday, we saw that Jesus **knew** what Peter would do before it happened. What did Jesus say Peter would do? (*Deny knowing Jesus three times.*) Was Jesus right? (*Yes*)

Earlier, Jesus had said something else about what would happen in the future:

The Son of Man (Jesus) will be handed over to the chief priests and teachers of the law. They will condemn Him to death and turn Him over to the Gentiles (non-Jews) to be mocked and whipped and crucified.

READ

Again Jesus was right! Read how His words came true in **John 18v28-32**.

TALK

Who did the Jewish leaders take Jesus to? (*Pilate, the Roman governor.*) Why did they take Jesus to Pilate? (v31) (*They wanted to have Jesus killed, but were not allowed to put anyone to death themselves.*) What does v32 tell us about Jesus? (*He was in charge! This happened to make His words come true.*)

THINK

This was exactly what Jesus had said would happen. Somehow it was all part of God's plan!

PRAY

Dear God, we don't always understand why things happen. Thank You that we can still trust You because Your plans always work out.

Building up
Read v28 again. These Jewish leaders were very careful in keeping <u>some</u> laws. They wouldn't enter the home of a non-Jewish person like Pilate during the Passover feast-time. But they weren't so bothered about <u>other</u> laws—like breaking all the rules about fair trials!

DAY 26
Captured king

KEYPOINT
Pilate asked who Jesus is. Jesus is God's chosen King, who came to rescue His people.

Today's passages are:
Table Talk: John 18v33-40
XTB: John 18v33-40

TABLE TALK

(*You need pencil and paper.*) Write 'Who is Jesus?' in the middle of paper. Then write or draw some possible answers. (*eg: He's a man born 2000 years ago; He's God's Son; He's the Christ; He's a miracle maker...*)

READ

The Jewish leaders had taken Jesus to Pilate, the Roman governor. They wanted him to put Jesus to death. **Read John 18v33-40**

TALK

What did Pilate ask Jesus? (v33) ('*Are you the King of the Jews?*') The Jewish leaders wanted Pilate to think that Jesus was a soldier king, who had come to <u>fight</u> the Romans. But Jesus said He wasn't that kind of king (v36). What <u>had</u> He come to do? (v37) (*To tell people the truth.*)

THINK

Do <u>you</u> believe the truth about Jesus? That He is the King of all God's people (Christians) and that He now rules as their King in heaven? Why/why not?

READ

The people outside Pilate's palace <u>didn't</u> believe that Jesus was the King who had come to rescue people from sin.
Read John 18v38-40

Who did they want set free instead of Jesus? (v40) (*The criminal Barabbas.*)

PRAY

Ask God to help you believe the truth about Jesus. Remember, He is the King of heaven who is in charge of you. What difference will that make to how you live?

Building up
King Jesus is now ruling in heaven. Use your **Bible Timeline** to see <u>when</u> He went back to heaven. What is the special name for this? (*Ascension*)

DAY 27
King of pain

KEYPOINT
Jesus was God's Son. Everything that happened was part of God's plan.

Today's passages are:
Table Talk: John 19v6-16
XTB: John 19v1-16

TABLE TALK

Copy these letters onto eight small pieces of paper, and hide them round the room: **D, F, G, N, O, O, O, S**. Ask your child to find the letters and put them together to make a title for Jesus. (*Son of God*)

READ

Yesterday, we saw how Pilate asked Jesus if He was the king of the Jews. But now Jesus was being accused of saying He was the Son of God as well...
Read John 19v6-16

TALK

What did the people shout? (v6) ('*Crucify Him*'.) Crucifixion meant being nailed to a wooden cross and left to die. Why didn't Pilate want to crucify Jesus? (v6) (*Jesus had done nothing wrong.*) But why did the Jewish leaders want Jesus crucified? (v7) (*Because He'd said He was the Son of God.*)

DO

They refused to believe that Jesus was God's Son. But God had clearly said that Jesus was His Son. When?—check it out on your **Bible Timeline**.

Who had given Pilate his power and authority? (v11) (*God*) Everything that was happening was part of <u>God's</u> plans!

PRAY

Thank God that He is in control of everything. Ask Him to help you really believe that Jesus is His Son who died to rescue you.

Building Up
Read John 19v1-5 The Roman soldiers didn't believe that Jesus was a king. So what did they do? (v2) (*Put a purple robe on Him, gave Him a crown of thorns, and pretended to bow down to Him.*) Check the speech bubble in Day 25's Table Talk. This is exactly what Jesus said would happen!

DAY 28
Cross words

KEYPOINT
When Jesus was crucified, the sign on His cross read 'Jesus of Nazareth, King of the Jews'.

Today's passages are:
Table Talk: John 19v17-22
XTB: John 19v17-22

PRAY

Jesus had done nothing wrong, yet He was sentenced to death. But remember, it was all part of **God's plan to rescue people!** Before you read today's verses, thank Jesus for going through so much to rescue you.

 READ **Read John 19v17-22**

Jesus was nailed to a wooden cross and was left to die. What was written on the sign on Jesus' cross? (v19) (*Jesus of Nazareth, the King of the Jews.*) What languages was it written in? (v20) (*Aramaic [Hebrew], Latin & Greek.*) This meant that everyone watching would know what the sign said.

Who didn't like what the sign said? (v21) (*The chief priests.*)

 TALK

The Jewish leaders were furious that Jesus was called their king. But Jesus **was** their King and not only their King, but the King of **everything**!

 THINK

King Jesus died on the cross to rescue people from their sin. If you really mean it, ask Jesus to be the King in charge of every part of your life.

 PRAY

Building up
Jesus was born in Bethlehem. But Mary and Joseph had to flee from there to Egypt to escape King Herod's plan to kill the young Jesus. When they returned to Israel, they settled in Nazareth in Galilee (the north of Israel). **Read Matthew 2v19-23**.

DAY 29
Amazing love

KEYPOINT
The soldiers gambled for Jesus' clothes—as Psalm 22 predicted. Jesus told John to care for Mary.

Today's passages are:
Table Talk: John 19v23-27
XTB: John 19v23-27

 TABLE TALK

Someone watching Jesus dying on the cross would have thought He was helpless. But as today's verses show, He was still in complete control!
Read John 19v23-24

 THINK

Jesus was dying on the cross and these soldiers were gambling for His clothes! Casting lots means throwing dice to see who would get the clothes. BUT flick back to **Psalm 22v18** to see that this was always part of God's plan.

 DO

God helped King David to write the words in this psalm many years before they came true. Use your **Bible Timeline** to find out how many years before. (*David lived 1000 years before Jesus.*)

 READ

Jesus was in agony—but that didn't stop Him caring for His mother and making sure she would be looked after. **Read John 19v25-27**

 THINK

How can you follow Jesus' example? Think of someone you could be more loving towards, and how you'll do it.

 PRAY

Jesus loves and cares for you too. Ask Him to help you be more loving to the person you thought about.

Building up
There are more verses in **Psalm 22** that point forward to Jesus' death. Read the whole psalm and see how many you can spot. (eg: v1, v6-8, v12-15, v17-18, v31.)

The end for Jesus?

KEYPOINT
When Jesus died, His work of rescuing His people from their sins was finished.

Today's passages are:
Table Talk: John 19v28-30
XTB: John 19v28-30

We're reading about the most important thing that's ever happened!
Read John 19v28-30

What were Jesus' last words before He died? (v30) ('*It is finished.*') What three things were finished...?

1. Old Testament prophecies (v28) Read **Psalm 69v21**. 1000 years before it happened, King David said that Jesus would be given vinegar to drink. It came true! The last prediction about Jesus' death had come true. Now it was time for Jesus to give up His life.

2. Jesus' suffering
Jesus suffered so much for people like you and me. He even took God's anger and punishment for us! All of that suffering was now finished.

3. Jesus' work
Jesus came to earth to rescue people from sin. This work as our Rescuer was now finished.

Use **Notes for Parents** opposite to see <u>how</u> Jesus' death on the cross can rescue us from our sin.

'It is finished' means that nothing else needed to be done to rescue us from our sins. Jesus had done it all!

What do you want to say to Him now?

Building up
Read Jesus' own words, explaining why He came in **John 3v16**. This is the most famous verse in the Bible. Learn it together as a memory verse.

Notes for Parents

GOD'S RESCUE PLAN
(You need pencil & paper.) *Prepare three separate pieces of paper. Write* **GOD** *on one,* **SIN** *on a second, and draw a person (a stick man is fine) on the third.*

Place the pieces of paper as shown.

ASK: *WHAT IS SIN?*
Sin is more than just doing wrong things. We all like to be **in charge** of our own lives. We do what **we** want instead of what **God** wants. This is called **sin**.

ASK: *WHAT DOES SIN DO?*
As the picture shows, **sin** gets in the way between us and God. It stops us from knowing God and from being His friends. Sin is a H-U-G-E problem—and there is nothing **we** can do about it.

But the great news is that Jesus came as our Rescuer, to <u>save</u> us from our sin. When Jesus died on the cross He was being punished. He took the punishment that we deserve, so that we can be forgiven.

Take the paper saying SIN and tear it in half. Then place the two halves as shown.

ASK: *WHAT GETS IN THE WAY NOW BETWEEN PEOPLE AND GOD?*
(Answer: *Nothing!*)

When Jesus died, He dealt with the problem of sin so that we can be forgiven. There is <u>nothing</u> to separate us from God any more. This was **God's Rescue Plan** for us.

Jesus did all this for us. What wonderful love!

DAY 31
Seeing is believing

KEYPOINT
John is a witness that Jesus really did die.

Today's passages are:
Table Talk: John 19v31-37
XTB: John 19v31-37

TABLE TALK

Ask your child to tell you about something they have seen (maybe at school) that you haven't seen. Explain that they are an eye-witness.

READ

A **witness** tells people what he or she saw to convince them about something. John is telling us what he saw when Jesus died... **Read John 19v35**

Why has John told us what he saw? (v35) (*So that we may believe.*)

READ

Now read the whole passage to see what John wants us to believe.
Read John 19v31-37

TALK

When people were crucified, their legs were sometimes broken so they would die quickly. Why weren't Jesus' legs broken? (v33) (*Because He was already dead.*) What did the soldiers do instead? (v34) (*Stuck a spear in Jesus' side, which was a way of checking He was really dead.*) Why did these things happen? (v36-37) (*So that the Old Testament words about Jesus would come true.*)

THINK

It's very important that Jesus really was dead. If Jesus didn't really die, then He also wasn't raised back to life and He can't rescue us from sin. But Jesus did die, and He is our Rescuer.

PRAY

John was a **witness** to Jesus' death. Do you believe what he tells you about Jesus? Ask God to help you believe everything the Bible tells you about Jesus.

Building up
Check out the Old Testament prophecies in
Psalm 34v20 and **Zechariah 12v10**.

DAY 32
Sneaking at night

KEYPOINT
Joseph and Nicodemus took Jesus' body, wrapped it in linen and buried Him in a stone tomb.

Today's passages are:
Table Talk: John 19v38-42
XTB: John 19v38-42

TABLE TALK

Jesus was crucified on a Friday. What do we call it? (*Good Friday*) The next day, Saturday, was the Jewish day of rest called the Sabbath. The Sabbath actually started at sunset on a Friday evening, which meant Jesus' body had to be moved quickly because no one was allowed to go near a dead body on the Sabbath. **Read John 19v38-42**

READ

TALK

Who asked Pilate for Jesus' body? (v38) (*Joseph of Arimathea*) Who helped Joseph? (v39) (*Nicodemus*) Both of these men were secret followers of Jesus, but now they boldly asked for the body and took Jesus to be buried.

What did they wrap Jesus' body in? (v40) (*Strips of linen cloth, with spices to keep the body smelling nice.*) Where did they bury Jesus? (v41) (*In a new tomb, in a garden near where Jesus had been killed.*) Then the tomb, which was cut out of the rock, was sealed with a large stone. Afterwards, Joseph and Nicodemus would have had to leave, because the Sabbath was beginning.

THINK

Not many people could have done what Joseph and Nicodemus did for Jesus. What things can you do for Jesus? (*eg: live the way He wants you to, tell others about Him...*)

PRAY

Ask God to help you do these things for Jesus.

Building up
Read about the time when Nicodemus went to visit Jesus secretly. **Read John 3v1-17**.

DAY 33
Tomb raiders?

KEYPOINT
On Sunday morning the tomb was empty. The grave clothes were there—the body wasn't!

Today's passages are:
Table Talk: John 20v1-9
XTB: John 20v1-9

TABLE TALK

<u>Recap:</u> What day of the week did Jesus die on? (*A Friday*) Why did He have to be buried quickly? (*The Sabbath started at sunset.*) Where was He buried? (*In a stone tomb, in a garden.*)

READ

The Sabbath lasted throughout Saturday, which meant no one could visit the tomb until early on Sunday morning...
Read John 20v1-9

TALK

Who went to the tomb first? (v1) (*Mary Magdalene*) She ran to tell Peter and John ('the disciple Jesus loved') that someone had taken Jesus body! Peter and John ran to see for themselves. Who got there first? (v4) (*John*) Who was the first to go inside? (v6) (*Peter*)

What did they see in the tomb? (v7) (*The linen cloth that had been wrapped round the body. It was neatly folded.*) What <u>didn't</u> they see? (*Jesus' body*)

THINK

Read v9 again. The Scriptures (the Old T) said that Jesus would come back to life again. Jesus had said so too. But the disciples had not understood it. Do you sometimes find it hard to **understand** the Bible? Maybe you find some of it hard to **believe**?

What did John do when he saw that Jesus' body was missing from the tomb? (v8) (*He saw and believed.*)

PRAY

Ask God to help you **understand** what He's saying to you in the Bible. And to **believe** what the Bible says.

Building up
Some people think robbers took the body. Why is this untrue? (*They wouldn't have unwrapped Him, and left the valuable cloth neatly folded up!*)

DAY 34
Big surprise!

KEYPOINT
Jesus was alive again! He met Mary, and gave her a message for His disciples.

Today's passages are:
Table Talk: John 20v10-18
XTB: John 20v10-18

TABLE TALK

When Mary Magdalene went to the tomb on Easter Sunday morning, what do you think she <u>expected</u> to find? (*The tomb sealed up, with Jesus' body inside it.*) What did she actually find? (*The stone had been moved and the body gone.*)

READ

Mary didn't expect an empty tomb. She also didn't expect to meet some angels!
Read John 20v10-13

TALK

Where were the angels? (v12) (*In the tomb, sitting where the body had been.*) What did Mary tell them? (v13) (*Someone had taken Jesus' body.*)

READ

But then Mary had an even greater shock... **Read John 20v14-18**

Who was standing behind Mary? (v14) (*Jesus*) Who did Mary think He was? (v15) (*The gardener.*) But as  soon as Jesus said her name, Mary realised who it was. She was so happy! Jesus was alive!!!

Jesus told Mary to tell the disciples that He would soon be going back to heaven. Did she? (v18) (*Yes*)

PRAY

Mary had been **sad**. But now she was so **happy** that Jesus was alive! Are <u>you</u> excited that Jesus is alive? It means He can help you now and, one day, take you to live for ever in heaven. Ask God to help you be excited about Jesus.

Building up
Grab your **Bible Timeline** and look at the section about the life of Jesus. Mark '**X**' on the line where you think Mary met the risen Jesus.

Heading for Heaven

Heaven is a wonderful place

filled with glory and grace

I want to see my Saviour's face

heaven is a wonderful place

I wanna go there...

Heaven is what, ultimately, the Gospel is all about. The big picture of the story of the human race starts with Creation, and finishes with the New Creation. The bit in the middle is about what went wrong, and how our loving God has amazingly put it right through Jesus.

But it is very easy to lose this focus. As a busy parent, you most probably don't have the time to think about tomorrow, let alone eternity. There's just so much to be done, so many things to be organised, so many pressing problems that need our attention NOW!

And children too are the same, if not more so. The immediate is what dominates their thinking, and it is part of our job as parents to help children understand some of the complex trade offs that we have to make as we grow older. The pain of regular music practice, so that they will acquire a skill that gives them joy throughout life. Saving money, so that they will be able to buy more valuable things in the future. Denying ourselves now, so that we can reap rewards later.

Christians in general have tended to lose this focus on heaven—partly because it seems a little 'super-spiritual' and not practical. Partly because of the pressing needs of our world and the increasing pace of our hectic lives. We need to recover it; and we need to help our children develop 'the big picture' for their lives too. Because if we do not see the

final goal properly, we are in danger of running the race in vain. It would be like driving through life without ever looking through the front windscreen, or bothering to check the map for the way to our destination.

WHAT IS HEAVEN?

There is a lot of confusion in people's minds about what heaven is. We have images of people floating around on clouds in nighties playing harps and smiling peacefully. Many children think that they will become angels when they die. Needless to say both these images are wrong—the Bible vision of eternity is far more amazing and wonderful.

John's revelation of heaven (see days 61 onwards in this issue of Table Talk), talks about a New Heaven and a New Earth being made. After the judgement day, the WHOLE UNIVERSE will be remade as a place where those who have been saved by Jesus will live forever. And notice (Rev 21v2) it is not <u>we</u> who will go up to heaven, but rather <u>heaven</u> that will come down to us!

WHAT'S IT LIKE?

The picture is painted of a place where there will be 'no more crying or grief or pain' and people living in harmony. But the most important thing is that **Jesus** will be in the centre of it. It is a remade version of the Garden of Eden, flourishing with abundance and good things. At its centre is a remade version of the Holy City, Jerusalem. And at the centre of the city is the the Lord God and Lord Jesus (21v22). It will be a place without sin, and a place of fulfilment, and fruitfulness.

This is where words fail and pictures take over. The new creation will be so amazingly different, that we are given many exciting images to whet our appetite: it is like a great party (Luke 14v15-24); a marvellous wedding feast (Matthew 22v1-14). Everything we are able to understand about it tells us that it will be utterly fantastic.

It will be important for you to think hard about how you talk about heaven with your children. The false versions seem boring and bland. The pull of what we can see and taste and enjoy will put the reality of heaven into the back of our minds. I made a private promise to myself to try and think about heaven at least once a day. I have also tried to talk about heaven as much as I can to my children—being enthusiastic about how wonderful it will be to see Jesus. How great it will be to not be troubled by my anger or my selfishness. How marvellous it will be to walk and talk, as Adam did, in the garden with my loving Lord. Every time I look at a cloud, I remind myself that the Lord Jesus will one day come on the clouds in great glory and take me home with him.

WHO WILL GO THERE?

Everything that is good will be in heaven. Everything that is bad will be excluded. (Revelation 21v8) No one qualifies for heaven by being good—because we simply can't be good enough. The only people there will be those who have been forgiven through the death the Lamb—Jesus Christ.

This raises an issue with children, especially when someone—perhaps a grandparent—dies. The rule here is that we must never say what we do not know. We can be certain if someone has loved Jesus in this life that they will be in Heaven. But for those who had no clear faith, we must never say where they will go. That's God's job—and He is very good at it! We can say for certain that God will do exactly the right thing—and that everyone will agree that He has done the right thing.

Children also worry about whether their pets will be in heaven. I know that it's easiest just to say 'yes', but that is not the most helpful answer in the long run. Again, we must

work from what we <u>know</u>, not what we don't know. Some of the Old Testament pictures of heaven include animals (see Isaiah 11v6-9). But we don't know if any *specific* animal will be in the new creation. What we do know is that everything that is *good* will be there. This is an opportunity for you to talk about all the things that you enjoyed in your pet. The fun you had playing with the hamster; the funny things the cat used to do; or, in our case, the hilarious way Betty the Hen used to jump up for food. All the good that we experienced in these things will be in heaven. And no one who is there will be in the least bit disappointed.

THE RESULT

The key thing to share with your children, of course, is the absolute necessity of making sure that they don't miss out. Pray that they would so fall in love with the Lord Jesus that they would long to be there with Him. Pray that they should so hunger and thirst after righteousness that they can't wait to be in heaven to be away from the sin that clings so closely.

And children who grow up knowing they are heading for heaven, will be the kind of people who are able to cope with whatever life throws at them. They will be prepared to be different, and march to the drum beat of eternity. They will not chase after the things of this world, but be prepared to live for Christ—even suffer and die—to bring the message to others. And it starts with you...

Tim Thornborough

> The new creation will be so amazingly different, that we are given many exciting images to whet our appetite: it is like a great party; a marvellous wedding feast. Everything we are able to understand about it tells us that it will be utterly fantastic.

DAY 35
Spread the news

KEYPOINT
Jesus appeared to His disciples and proved He was alive. He told them to tell others about Him.

Today's passages are:
Table Talk: John 20v19-23
XTB: John 20v19-23

TABLE TALK
Take it in turns to greet each other in different ways (*eg: Hello, G'day, Nice to meet you, Bonjour...*)

READ
In Bible times, one way of saying hello was to say 'Peace be with you.'
Read John 20v19-23

TALK
Why were the disciples meeting in a locked room? (v19) (*They were afraid of the Jewish leaders, who had put Jesus to death.*) Even though the doors were locked, who suddenly appeared in the room? (v19) (*Jesus*) It must have been hard for the disciples to believe that Jesus really was alive again. What did He show them? (v20) (*His hands, scarred from being nailed to the cross, and His side, which had been pierced by a spear.*)

What did Jesus say twice to His friends? (*Peace be with you.*) That meant *hello* in those days. But Jesus really can bring us **peace**. He can give us peace with God and rescue us from sin.

THINK
What else did Jesus say? (v21) (*As the Father has sent me, I am sending you.*) Everyone who has been rescued by Jesus has a job to do. They must tell others about Jesus and how He can forgive their sins. And Jesus gives them the Holy Spirit to help them do it! (v22).

PRAY
See **Notes for Parents** opposite for prayer (and action!) ideas.

Building up
The Holy Spirit helped Jesus' followers to tell others about Him. **Read Acts 1v8**.

TALKING ABOUT JESUS

Do you find it hard to tell your friends about Jesus? Here are some ideas you might try:

TELL THEM A STORY...
How about telling them a favourite Bible story about Jesus? (It may be one you've just read in John's Gospel.) Then tell them why it's your favourite.

ASK THEM WHAT THEY THINK...
Ask them who they think Jesus is. (And listen to their answer!) Then tell them who you believe Jesus is, and why. You could show them some evidence from John's Gospel (*eg: explain that the miracles are like signposts pointing to who Jesus is, then show them some of His miracles.*)

TALK ABOUT BEING A CHRISTIAN...
Tell them how it feels to have Jesus as your friend. Be honest about the things you find hard as well as the joy that comes from knowing that Jesus is your friend.

What happened with that hassle at school?

Well, er, I talked to God about it and an amazing thing happened...

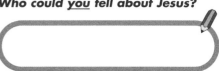

INVITE THEM TO COME WITH YOU...
Invite them to come to church or a Christian group with you. If getting there would be difficult, offer to pick them up, and maybe give them a meal afterwards.

Who could you tell about Jesus?

Now pray for them, and ask God to help you tell them about Jesus. **He will!**

DAY 36
Believe it or not?

KEYPOINT
Thomas wouldn't believe that Jesus was alive until he saw Jesus for himself.

Today's passages are:
Table Talk: John 20v24-31
XTB: John 20v24-31

TABLE TALK

Recap: What happened in the locked room? (*Jesus appeared to His disciples, and showed them His hands and side.*)

READ

But one of the disciples wasn't there. **Thomas** didn't see Jesus...
Read John 20v24-29

TALK

At first, did Thomas believe them? (*No*) Why not? (v21) (*He hadn't seen and touched Jesus for himself.*) In the end, what did Thomas say? (v28) (*'My Lord and my God.'*) At last, Thomas believed that Jesus was alive and was God's Son—but only because he **saw** Him.

THINK

You and I can't see or touch Jesus! So how can we believe that He's God's Son, alive forever? (*By reading what the eye-witnesses have written in the Bible.*)

Read John 20v30-31

Why did John write about the amazing things Jesus did? (v31) (*So that we may believe that Jesus is the Son of God.*)

PRAY

Thank God for giving us the true story of Jesus, written by His followers. Ask Him to help you read and believe it.

Building up

Jesus' followers wrote down what they had seen Jesus do. Many of them were killed for this! One of them, Luke, wrote Luke's Gospel and the book of Acts. Read what he says about this in **Luke 1v1-4** and **Acts 1v1-3**.

DAY 37
Fish for breakfast

KEYPOINT
The disciples tried to go back to their old job. But they were meant to catch people—not fish!

Today's passages are:
Table Talk: John 21v1-14
XTB: John 21v1-14

TABLE TALK

What was Peter's job before he became a disciple? (*Fisherman*) Do you know how they caught fish? (*Throwing nets from a boat. They fished at night, not the day.*)

READ

Jesus died, but God raised Him back to life! Wonderful! But what should the disciples do now? **Read John 21v1-3**

TALK

Peter suggested they all go fishing that night. How many fish did they catch? (v3) (*None!*) Who was waiting for them on the shore? (v4) (*Jesus*) What did He tell them to do? (v6) (*Throw their nets out on the right side of the boat.*) How many fish did they catch? (v11) (*153!*)

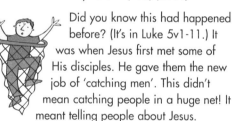

Did you know this had happened before? (It's in Luke 5v1-11.) It was when Jesus first met some of His disciples. He gave them the new job of 'catching men'. This didn't mean catching people in a huge net! It meant telling people about Jesus.

But what were they trying to catch now? (v3) (*Fish*) The disciples were happy that Jesus was alive. But now they wanted to go back to normal life—catching fish.

THINK

What would this miracle remind them of? (*The previous time Jesus did this and the new job He gave them.*) They couldn't go back to 'normal' life. They had to catch people, not fish!

PRAY

Are you as keen to tell people about Jesus as you used to be? Ask God to help you keep doing this and not give up. (*The ideas in Notes for Parents will help.*)

Building up
Read about the first fishy catch in **Luke 5v1-11**.

DAY 38
Feed my sheep

KEYPOINT
Jesus forgave Peter for denying Him and gave Peter the job of caring for Jesus' followers.

Today's passages are:
Table Talk: John 21v15-17
XTB: John 21v15-17

TABLE TALK

Quick Quiz: Who was known as Simon Peter or sometimes just Simon? (*Peter*) Who tried to fight back when Jesus was arrested? (*Peter*) Who said, three times, that he didn't know Jesus? (*Peter*) In yesterday's story, who suggested the disciples went fishing? (*Peter*)

READ

Peter must have felt <u>rotten</u> about denying Jesus. So Jesus had a talk with him...
Read John 21v15-17

TALK

What did Jesus ask Peter? (*'Do you love me?'*) How many times did Jesus ask Peter if he loved Him? (*Three times.*) Why do you think Jesus asked three times? (*Because Peter had denied Jesus three times.*)

Jesus was showing Peter that He **forgave** him! We all mess up and let Jesus down sometimes. But we can say sorry to Jesus and He will forgive us. Then we can get back to living in a way that pleases Jesus.

THINK

What did Jesus tell Peter to do? (v17) (*'Feed my sheep.'*) Hmm... do you think Peter was to look after white, woolly animals??? (*No!*) So what did Jesus mean? (*Jesus sometimes called His followers 'sheep': eg John 10v14-15. Peter was to look after Jesus' followers.*)

PRAY

Thank You Jesus that You love Your followers and forgive them when they let You down. Please help us to live to serve You. Amen

Building up
Read about Jesus our Shepherd in **John 10v10-16**.

DAY 39
Tough times ahead

KEYPOINT
Jesus told Peter he would be killed for following Jesus. But his death would bring glory to God.

Today's passages are:
Table Talk: John 21v18-19
XTB: John 21v18-24

TABLE TALK

Is there anything you would be willing to die for? (*eg: to save the life of someone you love.*)

READ

Jesus had forgiven Peter and given him a new job to do. What did 'Feed my sheep' mean? (*Take care of Jesus' followers.*) Then Jesus told Peter that he would end up <u>dying</u> for Jesus. **Read John 21v18-19**

TALK

Verse 18 means that Peter would be killed for following Jesus. What would his death bring? (v19) (*Glory to God.*)

THINK

Peter became a great leader, telling thousands of people about Jesus. But he was killed for it. Following Jesus isn't easy! People will tease you and hassle you. In some countries, people are even killed for following Jesus.

DO

Check out on your **Bible Timeline** what will happen to <u>all</u> Christians in the end. (*We'll live with God for ever in heaven.*)

PRAY

Dear God, please help us to serve You, even if we get hassle for it. Help Christians today who could be killed for following You. Thank You that we can look forward to living for ever in heaven with You.

Building up
Peter asked Jesus what would happen to John (the 'disciple Jesus loved'). **Read John 21v20-24** Jesus told Peter not to worry about John. What was Peter to concentrate on? (v22) (*Following Jesus.*) Ask God to help you not to get too wrapped up in what other people do, but to concentrate on living God's way.

KEYPOINT
John couldn't write down <u>everything</u> Jesus did—there wouldn't be room!

Today's passages are:
Table Talk: John 21v25
XTB: John 21v25

TABLE TALK

Collect a few books together, and count how many pages they each have. Why are the long books so much longer than the short ones? (*eg: because of the kind of book they are.*)

READ

Now count the number of pages in John's Gospel. It's quite a long book—but it could have been much l-o-n-g-e-r...
Read John 21v25

TALK

What would have happened if John wrote down <u>everything</u> Jesus did and said? (*There wouldn't have been room for all the books!*)

Do you remember why John wrote his book? (The clue is in John 20v31.) (*So that we believe that Jesus is the Christ, the Son of God, and that by believing we may have life in His name.*)

THINK

John wants us to **believe** that Jesus is the Christ (that means God's chosen King who can rescue us from sin), so that we can live with Him as King of our lives.

PRAY

Do <u>you</u> believe that Jesus is God's great Rescuer? Is He the King in charge of your life? Talk to God about your answers.

Building up
Use **Notes for Parents** opposite to remind yourselves of some of the signposts in John's Gospel.

SIGNPOSTS

The seven miracles in John's book are **signposts** pointing to <u>who</u> Jesus is.

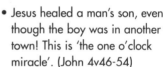

- At a wedding in Cana, Jesus turned water into wine. This was His first miracle. (John 2v1-11)

- Jesus healed a man's son, even though the boy was in another town! This is 'the one o'clock miracle'. (John 4v46-54)

- Then Jesus healed a man who'd been unable to walk for 38 years! (John 5v1-9)

- When a huge crowd followed Jesus up a hill, He fed them all with one boy's packed lunch! (John 6v1-13)

- Later that evening, Jesus walked across water to join His disciples in their boat. (John 6v16-21)

- Jesus healed a man who had been blind all his life. (John 9v1-41)

- Lazarus and his sisters Mary and Martha were friends of Jesus. When Lazarus died it seemed like the end—but Jesus brought him back to life again! (John 11v1-44)

DAYS 41–60
Notes for Parents

HISTORY HOP
*Find each person or event on your **Bible Timeline** as you read about them.*

• **Abraham**
God promised to give Abraham a HUGE family. They were called the Israelites.

• **Moses**
The Israelites were <u>slaves</u> in Egypt. But God rescued them (with Moses as their leader) and gave them the land of Canaan to live in.

• **Judges**
For 400 years the Israelites had judges to lead them. But then they demanded a king of their own (even though <u>God</u> was their Real King!).

• **Kings**
1. <u>Saul</u> was the first king of Israel —but he turned away from God.
2. <u>David</u> was the best king they ever had. He loved God.

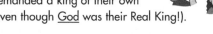

3. When David's son <u>Solomon</u> became king, he built a temple for God in Jerusalem. But later, Solomon turned away from God and worshipped pretend gods instead.

• **Exile**
God warned His people that if they turned away from Him they would be turned out of their country. (This is called exile.) But they didn't listen! So God allowed most of the Israelites to be captured by the Assyrians, and sent to live in far off countries.

• **Daniel**
The rest of the Israelites were captured by King Nebuchadnezzar of Babylon. They included Daniel and his friends S,M&A. Jerusalem was destroyed and the temple torn down.

DAY 41
History = His story

KEYPOINT
God's words always come true, both His warnings and His promises.

Today's passages are:
Table Talk: Ezra 5v11-16
XTB: Ezra 5v11-6

TABLE TALK
Today's we're going to start the last part of Old Testament history. So grab your **Bible Timeline** and use **Notes for Parents** to go for a History Hop!

READN
On Day 19, we saw Daniel praying that God would keep His promise to bring His people back to Jerusalem. God answered Daniel's prayer. The first group of Israelites came back to Jerusalem a few years later. We're going to dip into the book of Ezra to see what they said about themselves. **Read Ezra 5v11-16**

TALK
What were the Israelites rebuilding? (v11) (*God's temple*) Who had destroyed it? (v12) (*King Nebuchadnezzar*) But <u>who</u> had allowed King Neb to capture the Israelites and take them to Babylon? (v12) (*God*) Who told the Israelites to rebuild the temple? (v13) (*King Cyrus*)

King Cyrus of Persia <u>wasn't</u> one of God's people. But Ezra 1v1 tells us it was **God** who caused Cyrus to send the Israelites back to Jerusalem to rebuild the temple!

THINK
God had warned His people what would happen if they turned away from Him. But they didn't listen, so He sent them into exile. He also promised to bring them back 70 years later, and He did.
God's words always come true!

PRAY
Ask God to help you believe and obey His words as you read them in the Bible.

Building up
Read v14 again. Do you remember what King Belshazzar did with these temple goblets? It's in Daniel 5v1-31.

DAY 42
Bad news

Today's passages are:
Table Talk: Nehemiah 1v1-4
XTB: Nehemiah 1v1-4

TABLE TALK

As we saw yesterday, God had made King Cyrus of Persia send some of the Israelites back to Jerusalem to rebuild the temple. Many years later, some Israelites still lived in Persia. One of them was **Nehemiah**. He was a trusted servant of the king. Find Nehemiah on your **Bible Timeline**. Looking at the picture, what do you think Nehemiah is going to do?

READ

Nehemiah was waiting for his brother to come back from Jerusalem. He would have news of how the Israelites (Jews) who lived there were getting on...
Read Nehemiah 1v1-4

TALK

What was the news about... the <u>people</u>? (v3) (*They were in trouble.*) About the city <u>walls</u>? (v3) (*They were broken down.*) About the city <u>gates</u>? (v3) (*They were burnt.*) What did Nehemiah do when he heard this news? (v4) (*He wept; he didn't eat; he prayed.*)

Nehemiah was terribly upset—so he turned to God in prayer. *We'll read his prayer tomorrow...*

PRAY

God's people in Jerusalem were in great trouble, so Nehemiah <u>prayed</u> for them. Today there are some countries where God's people (Christians) are treated badly because they love Jesus. Pray for those Christians now. Ask God to be with them, and help them stand up for Him, even when that's hard.

Building up
Find out more about Christians who suffer because they follow Jesus. The Barnabas Fund (www.barnabasfund.org) is one place where you can find out more.

DAY 43
The way to pray

Today's passages are:
Table Talk: Nehemiah 1v4-11
XTB: Nehemiah 1v4-11

TABLE TALK

(*You need pen and paper.*) Write these four phrases on strips of paper: *Ask God for help; Tell God how great He is; Thank God for His promises; Confess the wrong things we've done.* Watch out for these four things as you read Nehemiah's prayer—and put them in the right order.

READ

Nehemiah had just heard that the Israelites in Jerusalem were in trouble, and that the city itself was in a terrible state. Nehemiah was so upset that he **wept** about it. But he also **prayed**...
Read Nehemiah 1v4-11

DO

Put the four strips of paper in the order that Nehemiah prayed them. Then write the matching verse numbers on each strip. (*God is great—v5; Confess—v6-7; God's promises—v8-9; Ask for God's help—v11.*)

TALK

What kind of help did Nehemiah ask for? (v11) (*Help when he asked the king a big favour.*) We'll see how God answered Nehemiah's prayer tomorrow...

PRAY

Pray together, using these same four steps. (Perhaps a different person could pray each part of the prayer.)

Building up
Read some of Jesus' teaching about prayer in **Matthew 6v5-13**.

DAY 44 Cupbearer to the king

KEYPOINT
God answered Nehemiah's prayers—both long and short.

Today's passages are:
Table Talk: Nehemiah 2v1-6
XTB: Nehemiah 2v1-6

 TABLE TALK

L—O—N—G Prayer

What Jewish month was it when Nehemiah heard the bad news about Jerusalem and its people? (Nehemiah 1v1) (*The month of Kislev.*) That was when Nehemiah started to pray.

What month was it by the start of chapter 2? (Nehemiah 2v1) (*The month of Nisan. Sadly the Good News Bible doesn't say this!*) Nisan was four months later than Kislev—but Nehemiah was still praying!

 THINK

If you're worried about something, don't just pray about it once! Keep praying, until you know what God's answer is.

SHORT Prayer

 READ

Nehemiah was a trusted servant, who served the king's wine. One day, God answered Nehemiah's prayers by giving him a chance to speak to the king... **Read Nehemiah 2v1-6**

 TALK

Why was the king surprised? (v1) (*Nehemiah looked so sad.*) When Nehemiah told the king about Jerusalem, the king asked what he wanted. What did Nehemiah do first? (v4) (*He prayed.*)

 THINK

Sometimes there isn't time for a l-o-n-g prayer. A quick prayer is fine—God already knows what you need!

God's answer this time was very quick. Did the king agree to Nehemiah's plans? (v6) (*Yes*)

 PRAY

You can pray anytime, anywhere, about anything! What do you want to talk to God about right now?

Building up
Check out **1 Thessalonians 5v16-18**.

DAY 45 Goodies and baddies

KEYPOINT
King Artaxerxes helped Nehemiah because God was with Nehemiah.

Today's passages are:
Table Talk: Nehemiah 2v6-10
XTB: Nehemiah 2v6-10

 TABLE TALK

Today we'll meet lots of people with odd names! But are they good guys or bad guys? *We'll find out...*

 READ

Nehemiah has just asked the king of Persia to let him go and rebuild Jerusalem. But it's a l-o-n-g way (two months travel!) and he'll need help... **Read Nehemiah 2v6-10**

Did King Artaxerxes agree that Nehemiah could go? (v6) (*Yes*)
Give the king a happy face.

The king also wrote letters to make sure that Nehemiah could travel safely, and would have the wood he needed to build with. (v7-8)
Draw happy faces for the governors of West Euphrates and Asaph the forest keeper.

How did Sanballat and Tobiah feel when they heard Nehemiah's plans? (v10) (*Upset and angry.*)
Draw angry faces for Sanballat and Tobiah.

 THINK

Why did Nehemiah get so much help from the king? (v8) (*God was with him, showing him great kindness.*)

 PRAY

Nehemiah had great plans for Jerusalem—but they only worked out because God was with him. Do you have plans to serve God? If they are His plans too, He will help you. Talk to Him about them now.

King Artaxerxes of Persia

Governors of West Euphrates

Asaph, keeper of royal forests

Sanballat the Horonite

Tobiah the Ammonite

DAY 46
Who said that?

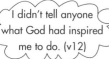

I didn't tell anyone what God had inspired me to do. (v12)

I told them how God had been kind to me. (v18)

Let us start rebuilding. (v18)

The God of heaven will give us success. (v20)

What is this you are doing? (v19)

READ

The speech and thought bubbles above come from today's verses. As you read the passage, spot who said or thought each one. **Read Nehemiah 2v11-20**

TALK

Who were Nehemiah's thoughts and words about? (v12, 18 & 20) (*God*) He knew that God had chosen him to rebuild Jerusalem, and that only God could help the people do it.

THINK

How quickly did the people agree to start rebuilding? (v18) (*Straight away.*) When you get the chance to do something for God, do you do it as soon as possible?

What did Sanballat and Tobiah do? (v19) (*Laughed at the Israelites.*)

When we do what God wants us to do, we will sometimes get laughed at—like these Israelites. But Nehemiah wasn't put off. Why not? (v20) (*He knew that God would give them success.*)

PRAY

God wants Christians to do His work and will help us if we ask Him. Don't be put off by people who tease you. Ask God to help you do what He wants.

Building up
There's a map of the city walls on the next page. The names won't be filled in until tomorrow, but you can still use it to trace Nehemiah's route in **v13-15**.

DAY 47
Sheep, fish & dung!

TABLE TALK

Recap: Which city had Nehemiah gone to? (*Jerusalem*) What had he examined in the night? (*The city walls.*) When Nehemiah asked the Israelites to start rebuilding the walls, did they agree? (*Yes*) How quickly? (*Straight away.*)

DO

Chapter 3 lists all the people who rebuilt the walls, and which bits they built. There's a **map** of the walls on the next page—but with some names missing! Look up the verse numbers on the map to fill in the names of the city gates that were rebuilt.

READ

Everyone got involved—except for a few lazy nobles! Check out these verses to see who helped:

v1 **P**_____

v3 **S**_____

v8 **G**_____

v8 **P**_____ **M**_____

v12 **D**_____

v26 **S**_____

v32 **M**_____

(Priests, sons, goldsmiths, perfume makers, daughters, servants, merchants.)

PRAY

Everyone can serve God. No one is too young or not important or gifted enough. If you tell God you want to serve Him, then He will give you ways to do it! If that's what you want to do, tell Him so now.

Building up
Jesus was a servant, and calls **us** to be servants too. **Read Mark 10v42-45**.

REBUILDING THE WALLS

This map shows the walls of Jerusalem at the time of Nehemiah. Look up the verse numbers to find the names of the city gates.

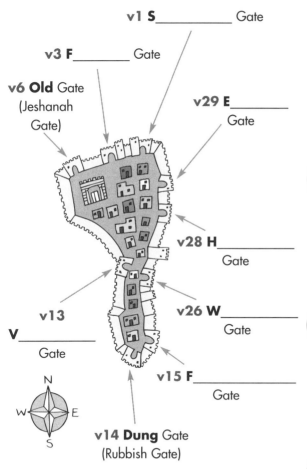

v1 **S**_____ Gate

v3 **F**_____ Gate

v6 **Old** Gate
(Jeshanah
Gate)

v29 **E**_____ Gate

v28 **H**_____ Gate

v13
V_____ Gate

v26 **W**_____ Gate

v15 **F**_____ Gate

v14 **Dung** Gate
(Rubbish Gate)

N · W · E · S

KEYPOINT
Nehemiah and the Israelites <u>prayed</u> a lot—and <u>did</u> a lot.

Today's passages are:
Table Talk: Nehemiah 4v14-20
XTB: Nehemiah 4v1-23

TABLE TALK

Some of Sally's schoolmates are teasing her for being a Christian. What should she do?

The Israelites were being laughed at by their enemies (v1-3).

What can those feeble Jews do with all that rubble?

Even a fox could knock that wall down!

READ

But when Nehemiah heard this he **prayed** about it, and the Israelites kept rebuilding the wall until it reached half its full height. Then their enemies plotted to attack Jerusalem! So the Israelites **prayed** to God for help. Some of the Israelites were afraid—but Nehemiah told them to remember how <u>great</u> God is...
Read Nehemiah 4v14-20

TALK

What did Nehemiah tell the people? (v14) (*Don't be afraid. Remember the Lord. Fight for your families.*) How were the people divided? (v16) (*Half did the work, and half were ready to fight.*) Nehemiah kept a trumpeter with him at all times. Why? (v20) (*To call the men to fight when needed.*) Who was going to fight as well? (v20) (*God!*)

THINK

Nehemiah and the Israelites **prayed** a lot—and **did** a lot too! **Prayer <u>and</u> action**. They knew they could only build the wall and beat their enemies if their great God helped them.

PRAY

When you have a problem, do you do the same? **Pray** and **do** something! Talk to God about anything that's bothering you.

Building up
Read the whole story in **Nehemiah 4v1-23**.

DAY 49
Rebuilding

KEYPOINT
Nehemiah didn't just rebuild the <u>walls</u>. The <u>people</u> needed rebuilding too!

Today's passages are:
Table Talk: Nehemiah 5v9 & 14-19
XTB: Nehemiah 5v1-19

TABLE TALK

What had Nehemiah been rebuilding? (*The walls of Jerusalem.*) But the walls were not the only thing that needed rebuilding! Play **hangman** to guess what else Nehemiah needed to rebuild. (*The answer is 'God's people'.*)

READ

The Israelites (Jews) in Jerusalem were <u>God's</u> people. But they weren't living the way <u>God</u> wanted them to! The **rich** rulers were taking advantage of the rest. The **poor** people had to sell their land and homes to these rulers. Some even sold their children as slaves! Nehemiah was very angry with the rich rulers...
Read Nehemiah 5v9

TALK

Who would see that the Israelites were not living God's way? (v9) (*Their non-Jewish [Gentile] enemies.*)

Unlike the rest of the people, Nehemiah <u>did</u> live God's way...
Read Nehemiah 5v14-19

Why didn't Nehemiah act like the previous governors? (v15) (*Out of respect for God.*)

THINK

This chapter gives us two top reasons for living God's way: **1**—Because other people see how we live (v9). **2**—Because we love and respect God. (v15)

PRAY

Ask God to help you live His way for these reasons.

Building up
Living God's way includes showing kindness to the poor. Talk about how you can do this. Then ask God to help you do it.

DAY 50
A trio of plots

KEYPOINT
Nehemiah's enemies couldn't stop the walls being finished. No one can stop God's plans!

Today's passages are:
Table Talk: Nehemiah 6v5-9 & 15-16
XTB: Nehemiah 6v1-16

TABLE TALK

Nehemiah's enemies were still trying to stop him from rebuilding the walls...

PLOT ONE (v1-4)

Come and meet us on the plain of Ono.

But Ono was a day's journey away, and Nehemiah knew the work would stop while he was gone. So he said 'Oh No' to Ono!

PLOT TWO (v5-9)

Next, Sanballat sent an <u>unsealed</u> letter (which meant everyone could read the lies written in it). **Read Nehemiah 6v5-9**

What did the letter say Nehemiah was planning to do? (v6) (*Revolt against the king of Persia and make himself king.*) But it wasn't true. Sanballat was making it all up! What was Sanballat trying to do? (v9) (*Frighten them.*) But what did Nehemiah do? (v9) (*He prayed.*)

PLOT THREE (v10-14)

Nehemiah's enemies got a pretend prophet to give him a message from God—to run and hide in the temple. But Nehemiah knew the man was lying, and wouldn't run away.

THE RESULT (v15-16)
Read Nehemiah 6v15-16
What was the result of all these plots? (*The wall was finished in only 52 days!*)

PRAY

Nehemiah's powerful enemies couldn't stop the wall being finished, because <u>God</u> was helping His people (v16). Thank God that nothing and no one can stop His plans.

Building up
Read the full details of Plots One and Three in **Nehemiah 6v1-4** and **6v10-14**.

DAY 51
Listen and learn

Today's passages are:
Table Talk: Nehemiah 8v1-8
XTB: Nehemiah 8v1-8

TABLE TALK

What two things had Nehemiah's been rebuilding? (*The walls and the people.*)

READ

The walls were finished. But the people weren't! They needed to know more about God and how He wanted them to live. That meant listening to God's Word... **Read Nehemiah 8v1-8**

DO

Which gate did the people meet at? (v1) (*The water gate.*) Find this on the **map** on Day 47.

TALK

Who read God's Word to the people? (v2) (*Ezra the priest.*) What did the people do? (v3) (*Listened attentively.*) What did the people say? (v6) (*Amen! Amen!*) **Amen** means 'so be it' or 'I agree'. We often say it at the end of a prayer to show that we agree with what was said.

THINK

Have you noticed that God's Word (the Bible) can sometimes be hard to understand? If the Israelites were going to rebuild their lives—to live as <u>God's</u> people—they needed help to understand what God was saying to them. Who helped them? (v7) (*The Levites—a group of Israelites who served God in His temple.*)

PRAY

Who helps <u>you</u> understand the Bible? Thank God for them and ask Him to help them to teach His Word clearly so that you and many others can know God.

Building up
Send a letter or card (and maybe a present!) to someone who teaches you the Bible. Thank them for what they do and tell them you've been praying for them.

DAY 52 Remember remember

Today's passages are:
Table Talk: Nehemiah 8v9-18
XTB: Nehemiah 8v9-18

TABLE TALK

If you can, do today's Table Talk <u>outside</u>. If not, at least meet in a different place to usual (sit on the floor if you have to!).

READ

The Israelites had spent <u>all</u> morning listening to God's Word. How do you think they felt? (*Tired? Happy? Bored?*) Read the verses to find out. **Read Nehemiah 8v9-12**

TALK

The people were <u>crying</u> as they heard God's Law, because they knew they hadn't kept it. They hadn't lived the way God wanted them to. But what did Nehemiah tell them? (v10) (*The joy of the Lord will make you strong.*)

READ

Nehemiah sent the people home to <u>celebrate</u> all that God had done for them. But the next day they came back to hear more from God's Word... **Read Nehemiah 8v13-18**

What did the people build? (v16) (*Shelters/booths.*)

The Festival of Shelters (or Booths or Tabernacles) was meant to be held every year. It reminded the Israelites of the time when God had rescued them from Egypt. As they travelled to the new land God had promised them, with <u>Moses</u> as their leader, they lived in temporary shelters or tents. After <u>Joshua</u> led them into Canaan, they settled into permanent homes. *Find **Moses** and **Joshua** on your Bible Timeline.*

PRAY

It's really important to remember the great things God has done for us. That's why we celebrate Christmas and Easter. What can you do this week to remind you of something God has done for you? Ask God to help you.

Building up
Read about the *Festival of Shelters* in **Leviticus 23v37-43**.

DAY 53
So-o-o sorry

KEYPOINT
The Israelites spent a quarter of a day praying! They were confessing and worshipping.

Today's passages are:
Table Talk: Nehemiah 9v1-6
XTB: Nehemiah 9v1-6

Read Nehemiah 9v1
What were the Israelites wearing? (*Sackcloth*) What did they put on their heads? (*Dust*) Do you know why? (*Sackcloth and dust were a way of showing sadness and sorrow.*) The Israelites were showing how sorry they were for disobeying God's laws.

Read Nehemiah 9v2-6

> You **alone** are the LORD.
> You made the **heavens**.
> You made all the **stars**.
> You made the **earth** and **seas**
> and everything in them.
> You give life to **everything**.

Find all the underlined bold words in the wordsearch. (Some are backwards!) Copy the leftover letters (in order) to spell two new words:

C _ _ _ _ _ _

W _ _ _ _ _ _

The people spent a quarter of the day (at least three hours!) praying. They were confessing (saying sorry to God) and worshipping (telling God He's great).

Use the same pattern to pray now. Say **sorry** to God (be specific), then tell Him how **great** He is (at least three reasons!).

```
C S R A T S S E A S
O N F E S A L O N E
G N I H T Y R E V E
H T R A E S W O R S
H E A V E N S H I P
```

DAY 54
You, You, You

KEYPOINT
The history of the Israelites is really all about <u>God</u>. History = His Story.

Today's passages are:
Table Talk: Nehemiah 9v7-15
XTB: Nehemiah 9v7-15

TABLE TALK

(*You need pen and paper.*) Write **YOU** on the paper. As you read the next part of the Israelites' prayer to God, put a tick on the paper every time you read '**You**' (which means <u>God</u>).

READ

Read Nehemiah 9v7-15

Wow! This prayer is all about **God**. How many ticks did you put? (*Over 20!*)

TALK

God chose **Abram** to be the start of the Israelites nation. What new name did God give to Abram? (v7) (*Abraham*) Abraham means 'father of many'. God promised to give Abraham a HUGE family—and He did! They were the Israelites.

DO

*Find **Abraham** on your **Bible Timeline**.*

Who promised to give Abraham's family a land of their own? (v7-8) (*God*) Who sent miracles to rescue the Israelites from Egypt? (v9-10) (*God*) Who made a dry path through the Red Sea? (v11-12) (*God*) At Mount Sinai, who gave laws to show them how to live as His people? (v13-14) (*God*) Who gave them food and water in the desert? (v15) (*God*)

THINK

Although this is the history of the Israelites—it's really all about <u>God</u>! ***History = His Story***.

PRAY

On your sheet of paper, write a history of <u>your</u> lives, showing how God has helped you. Then thank Him for these things.

Building up
Read God's promises to Abram in **Genesis 12v1-3, 15v13-14** and **17v1-8**.

DAY 55
But, but, but

KEYPOINT
The people had let God down badly. But He was still loving, kind and forgiving.

Today's passages are:
Table Talk: Nehemiah 9v16-21
XTB: Nehemiah 9v16-21

TABLE TALK

What word kept popping up in yesterday's verses? (*You*) Read a few of them again (eg: v6-8) and every time you read '**You**' your child must stand up, turn around, and sit down again!

READ

Yesterday's reading listed the great things God did for the Israelites. But today's reading starts with a very sad word: <u>But</u>...
Read Nehemiah 9v16-21

But they...
God had done <u>so</u> much for His people. They should have loved and obeyed Him. But they didn't! What were the Israelites like? (*See v16-17.*)

But God...
Even though the Israelites turned away from God, He was still loving and good. How is God described? (*See v17.*)

But today...
These things happened thousands of years ago. But God doesn't change! He is still loving, kind and forgiving today.

THINK

Sometimes you and I are like those Israelites. We turn away from God and don't keep His commands. But God is loving and forgiving. That's why He sent Jesus, so that we can be forgiven for our wrongs, and be friends with God again.

PRAY

Say sorry to God for anything you have done today that let Him down. Thank Him for sending Jesus so that you can be forgiven.

Building up
Verse 17 uses a description of God that was first spoken by God to Moses.
Read Exodus 34v4-6.

DAYS 56
Notes for Parents

HISTORY HOP (AGAIN!)

The prayer in chapter 9 is a short history of the Israelites:

- It starts with God's promises to
  A_____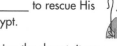

- The Israelites settled in Egypt at the time of
  J_____

- When they became slaves, God chose
  M_____ to rescue His people from Egypt.

  - After crossing the desert, it was
    J_____ who led the Israelites into the promised land of Canaan.

- But the people kept turning away from God, so He allowed their enemies to attack them. When the people cried out to God for help, He chose *judges* to rescue them.
  G_____ was one of those judges.

- Later, the people demanded a king—even though <u>God</u> was their Real King. Their first king was **S**_____
  —but he turned away from God.

  - **D**_____ was the best king of all. He loved God.

- When David's son
  S_____ became king,
  he built a great temple for God. But later, he turned away from God, and his kingdom became divided.

- The Israelites continued to disobey God's laws. So He allowed them to be captured by the Assyrians and the Babylonians. Some of them came back to Jerusalem at the time of
  N_____.

DAY 56
End to end

KEYPOINT
God was always <u>faithful</u> to the Israelites—even when they were <u>faithless</u>.

Today's passages are:
Table Talk: Nehemiah 9v33-37
XTB: Nehemiah 9v22-37

DO

Notes for Parents opposite shows how the history of the Israelites is summed up in Nehemiah chapter 9. *Use your **Bible Timeline** to fill in the gaps.*

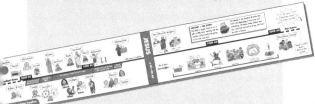

READ

In the last few days, we've seen how God was always **faithful** to the Israelites. (He always kept His promises.) But the Israelites were **faithless**. (They didn't keep theirs!) This is summed up in these verses: **read Nehemiah 9v33-37**

THINK

Read v33 again. Use your own words to sum up what this verse is saying about God, and about the Israelites.

PRAY

God is <u>always</u> faithful! Nothing you or I do can make God break His promises! He always does what is right and good. How does that make you feel? Talk to Him about it now.

Building up
God's character is always to be faithful, even when His people are not. See how Paul sums this up in **2 Timothy 2v11-13**.

DAY 57 An agreement with God

KEYPOINT
The Israelites made an agreement with God.

Today's passages are:
Table Talk: Nehemiah 9v38 & 10v28-29
XTB: Nehemiah 9v38–10v39

TABLE TALK

Yesterday, we learnt that nothing we do can make God break His promises. Does that mean it doesn't matter what we do or how we live? Why/why not?

The Israelites knew that God was loving and faithful. But this didn't mean they could just live as they pleased!
Read Nehemiah 9v38

What did the Israelites make? (v38) (*An agreement.*)

READ

This written agreement was between the Israelites and God...
Read Nehemiah 10v28-29

TALK

What were the Israelites agreeing to do? (v29) (*Keep God's laws.*) The people promised to live the way God wanted them to, and to look after His temple. (If you have time, read the full agreement in v30-39.) Who made this agreement? (v28) (*Everyone—including all the sons and daughters who were old enough to understand.*)

THINK

Are <u>you</u> ready to make this kind of agreement with God? Think carefully about it, and read the words below. Then if you want to, each sign your name at the bottom. (This is an important agreement, so don't worry if you're not ready. Ask God to help you to keep thinking about it until you are.)

AGREEMENT
Dear God, thank You that You are always loving and faithful. Thank You for the Bible that shows me how You want me to live. I commit myself to living Your way and keeping Your laws. Please help me to do this.
Signed:

New walls

Notes for Parents

KEYPOINT
The Israelites marched round the finished walls, full of the joy God gave them.

Today's passages are:
Table Talk: Nehemiah 12v40-43
XTB: Nehemiah 12v27-43

TABLE TALK

Do you like walking along walls? Have you ever walked on huge walls, round a walled city? (eg: York and Chester both have old Roman walls round them.)

READ

My mum and dad live in Chester, so I've walked round the walls of Chester loads of times. But not how Nehemiah did! Read the cartoon story in **Notes for Parents** to see how the Israelites walked round their walls.

Read Nehemiah 12v40-43

TALK

Where did the two choirs meet? (v40) (*The temple, called here the 'house of God'.*) What did the people give? (v43) (*Many sacrifices (gifts) to God.*) How did they feel? (v43) (*Full of joy—given to them by God.*) Where could the celebrations be heard? (v43) (*Far away.*)

THINK

At the beginning of Nehemiah's book, he was very sad because Jerusalem was in ruins. Now the city was rebuilt, with strong walls to protect it. No wonder the people were so full of joy!

PRAY

The people marched and sang to show their thanks to God. How can _you_ thank God today? Try and pick something you don't usually do—like singing, making something, having a celebration...

Building up
See **Notes for Parents** for today's **Building Up** section.

WALKING THE WALLS
(*Based on Nehemiah 12v27-40.*)

Nehemiah called together a huge crowd of singers and musicians.

They split into two large choirs... ...both standing on top of the new walls.

Ezra's group went **right**. Nehemiah's went **left**.

They walked all round the walls—singing praise and thanks to God.

Then they met up again at God's temple.

Building up
Verse 43 says that God gave His people joy. Joy isn't the same as being happy. Flick back to **Nehemiah 8v10** to see what Nehemiah said about joy. Compare this with **Romans 15v13**. Pray about what you've discovered.

DAY 59
Same old people

KEYPOINT
The people broke their agreement. They were still sinful, and Nehemiah couldn't change them.

Today's passages are:
Table Talk: Nehemiah 13v10-11, 15-16, 23-24
XTB: Nehemiah 13v10-24

TABLE TALK

Look at two photos of your child or family—one recent, one a few years old. What are the <u>differences</u> between the two? What things have stayed the <u>same</u>?

THINK

Nehemiah had been rebuilding two things—the **walls** and the **people**. The walls were finished. They were safe and strong. But what about the people???

On Day 57 we saw that the people made an **agreement** with God. They agreed:

Agreement

- Not to marry people who didn't follow God. (10v30)
- Not to buy or sell on God's rest day (the Sabbath). (v31)
- To give money and gifts for God's temple. (10v32-39)

READ

As you read today's verses, see which of these promises the people broke...

Read Nehemiah 13v10-11
What did the people stop doing? (*They stopped giving money to the temple.*)

Read Nehemiah 13v15-16
What did they do on the Sabbath? (*Buy and sell.*)

Read Nehemiah 13v23-24
Who did they marry? (*People who didn't follow God.*)

The people were **still sinful**—and Nehemiah couldn't change them!

PRAY

Jesus is the **only** person who can solve the problem of sin. (More about that tomorrow.) Think of anything you need to say sorry to God for. Then thank God for sending Jesus so that you can be forgiven.

Building up
Sin comes from <u>inside</u> us. Only Jesus can clean our sinful hearts. **Read Mark 7v20-23**.

DAY 60
The silence is broken

KEYPOINT
Nehemiah couldn't rebuild people—but Jesus can!

Today's passages are:
Table Talk: Matthew 1v18-21
XTB: Matthew 1v18-21

Nehemiah was a good leader who loved God. He did a great job of rebuilding the walls of Jerusalem. But he <u>couldn't</u> rebuild the people!

DO

Find **Nehemiah** on your **Bible Timeline**. What comes next on the timeline? (*400 years of silence.*)

All through the Old Testament, God had sent **messengers** (called prophets) to speak to the Israelites. But the people stopped <u>listening</u> to God...

...so He stopped <u>sending</u> His messengers.

READ

After 400 years, the silence was broken—in a town called Nazareth...
Read Matthew 1v18-21

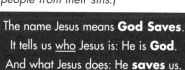

The angel told Joseph that Mary's baby was from God's Holy Spirit. What were they to call Him? (v21) (*Jesus*) Why? (v21) (*Because He will save His people from their sins.*)

The name Jesus means **God Saves**. It tells us <u>who</u> Jesus is: He is **God**. And what Jesus <u>does</u>: He **saves** us.

DO

(*Optional*) Copy this on to some paper and stick it where you'll all see it.

PRAY

Nehemiah couldn't rebuild people—but **Jesus** can! When we become His followers (Christians), Jesus changes us to become more and more like Him. Do you want to be like Jesus? (Loving God and other people, and keeping God's laws.) If you do, ask Him to change you.

Building up
Think back over the story of Nehemiah. What have you learnt about God? What have you learnt about living for God?

ALL REVEALED

The last book in the Bible is called **Revelation** because it <u>reveals</u> something that was hidden.

Revelation 1v1 tells us where this revelation came from:

> **God** gave it to **Jesus** who gave it to an **angel** who gave it to **John**.

Did you know?

This is the same **John** who wrote John's Gospel. John was one of Jesus' disciples. His older brother James was also a disciple. Their dad was called Zebedee!

John had got into trouble for telling people about Jesus. He was imprisoned on an island called Patmos. That's where he was when he wrote the book of Revelation, about the amazing things God's angel revealed to him.

Find **John's vision of heaven** on your **Bible Timeline**. (A vision is a kind of dream.)

Pray

What a fantastic promise! No one will be sad in heaven. No one will cry. If you're a Christian (a follower of Jesus) then this promise is for you! **Read v4 again**. Which part of this promise are you looking forward to the most? Tell God why, and then thank Him for the wonderful promise of heaven.

KEYPOINT
God will live with His people in heaven. No one will be sad there. No one will cry.

Today's passages are:
Table Talk: Revelation 21v1-4
XTB: Revelation 21v1-4

TABLE TALK
Hide two envelopes in the room—one with a hanky or tissue in it, the other containing a plaster. Ask your child to <u>find</u> the envelopes, but not <u>open</u> them.

Turn to the very <u>last</u> book in the Bible. What is it called? (*Revelation*) Find out more about **Revelation** by reading **Notes for Parents** together.

READ
We're going to read the last part of the book of Revelation. It's all about heaven...
Read Revelation 21v1-4

TALK
What did John see? (v1) (*A new heaven and a new earth.*) Where do these words come on your Bible Timeline? (*The end.*) These words are at the <u>end</u> of the timeline because Jesus will come back again one day and our world will end. John's vision shows us what that will be like.

1—What did John see coming down from heaven? (v2) (*A beautiful city.*) We'll find out about the city on Day 63.

2—Where will God live? (v3) (*With His people.*)

3—And <u>because</u> God will be living with His people, what <u>won't</u> be there? (v4) (*No death, mourning, crying or pain.*)

DO
Open the two envelopes to **reveal** what's inside. Why won't the things in the envelopes be needed in heaven? (*No pain means we won't need plasters. No crying means we won't need hankies!*)

PRAY
See **Notes for Parents** for today's prayer ideas.

Building up
Read the beginning of the book—Revelation 1v1-3.

DAY 62
Alpha and Omega

Today's passages are:
Table Talk: Revelation 21v5-8
XTB: Revelation 21v5-8

TABLE TALK

In <u>one minute</u>, how many words can you find beginning with **A** or **Z**? (*1-15: good try; 16-30: well done; 30+: superbrains!*)

A and **Z** are the first and last letters in our alphabet. The first and last letters in the **Greek** alphabet are called <u>Alpha</u> and <u>Omega</u>. They look like this:

Little Alpha   Little Omega   Capital Alpha   Capital Omega

READ

John heard **God** speaking from His throne. God called <u>Himself</u> the Alpha and the Omega... **Read Revelation 21v5-8**

TALK

What else does God call Himself? (v6) (*The first and the last/The beginning and the end.*) God has always existed and always will. He is the God of <u>all</u> time and history!

What does God give to those who live for Him? (v6) (*To drink the water of life. This means eternal life with God in heaven.*) Those who keep on living for God will be given (inherit) all the things John saw in his vision (v7). What will their relationship with God be like? (v7) (*He'll be their God and they'll be His children.*) But those who turn away from God will be thrown into hell (v8).

Are <u>you</u> a follower of Jesus?

PRAY

Yes?—thank God for His wonderful promise of eternal life with Him in heaven. Ask Him to help you tell your friends about Jesus too.

Not sure?—read **Notes for Parents** on Day 30.

Building up
The Bible uses frightening language to describe hell (eg: v8). Make sure your child knows that if they have put their trust in **Jesus** then they don't need to be scared of hell. Their place in <u>heaven</u> is certain. (John 3v36)

DAY 63
The holy city

Today's passages are:
Table Talk: Revelation 21v22-27
XTB: Revelation 21v9-27

The angel showed John a beautiful city.
Check out the verses to see what it was like.

The **wall** was made of j_____
(a precious stone). [Revelation 21v18]

The **city** was pure
g_____ . [Rev 21v18]

The **gates** were
p_____ . [Rev 21v21]

But some things were <u>missing</u> from the city...
Read Revelation 21v22-27

TALK

What was missing? (v22-23) (*No temple; no sun or moon.*) There will be no need for a special place to worship God because God the Father, and Jesus (called the Lamb), will be there with us. Their glory will be far brighter than any light—even the sun!

Are the gates open or shut? (v25) (*Open*) There's no need to shut the gates because nothing impure can enter the city (v27).

THINK

But this city is just a <u>picture</u> of heaven. There will be a whole new universe. Everything will be new and more wonderful than anyone can imagine!

PRAY

If you're a Christian, <u>your</u> name is in the **book of life** (v27) and you will live in heaven with God. Thank Him for this now.

Building up
Read Revelation 21v10-14. What names did the city have on it? (v12&14) (*The 12 tribes of Israel and the 12 apostles [disciples].*) This amazing city was a picture of God's people—from Old Testament times <u>and</u> New Testament times. **All** Christians, throughout history, will be inside this city!

DAY 64
Curse reverse

Today's passages are:
Table Talk : Revelation 22v1-6
XTB : Revelation 22v1-6

 TABLE TALK

At the very <u>beginning</u> of the Bible we meet these people.

*Check your **Bible Timeline** to see who they are.*

Adam and Eve disobeyed God. So all people were **cursed**. They were banned from eating from the **tree of life** and from living with God for ever. (Genesis 3)

 READ

At the very <u>end</u> of the Bible, John learns something wonderful about that **curse**...
Read Revelation 22v1-6

 TALK

What did John see? (v1-2) (*The river of the water of life, and the tree of life.*) And what's the great news? (v3) (*There will no longer be any curse.*) In heaven, God will <u>remove</u> His curse. His people will be allowed to eat from the tree of life and live for ever with Him!

 THINK

What do verses 3-5 tell us about God's people? (*v3—they will <u>serve</u> God. v4—they will <u>see His face</u>—nothing will separate God from His people. v4—<u>His name</u> will be on their foreheads—they will belong completely to God. v5—they will <u>reign</u> for ever—they're God's servants, but they'll also rule with Him!*)

 PRAY

What a lot to thank God for...
...so start right now!

Building up
Read about the original curse in **Genesis 3v16-24**. What separated Adam and Eve from the tree of life? (v24) (*Cherubim/heavenly creatures and a flaming sword.*) Thank God that Jesus has made it possible for us to eat from the tree of life.

DAY 65
Coming soon...

Today's passages are:
Table Talk : Revelation 22v12-16 & 20-21
XTB : Revelation 22v7-21

 TABLE TALK

(*You need pen and paper.*) Each word in this sentence has been jumbled up:
SEUJS SI MOCING NOSO. Copy it out and ask your child to unjumble it.

 READ

The last 15 verses of the Bible cover a mix of things. But one important fact comes up eight times—Jesus is coming soon!

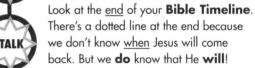 **TALK**

Look at the <u>end</u> of your **Bible Timeline**. There's a dotted line at the end because we don't know <u>when</u> Jesus will come back. But we **do** know that He **will**!

Read Jesus' own words about it...
Read Revelation 22v12-16

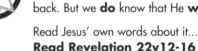

Jesus says there are **two** different types of people:

A: Some people have had their sins washed away by Jesus. They can enter God's city and live for ever with Him. (v14)

B: The rest continue to disobey Jesus. They will have to stay outside the city. They will be punished for ever. (v15)

Have <u>you</u> had your wrongs forgiven by Jesus? Will you live with Him for ever? If you're not sure, talk to an older Christian about it. It's hugely important!

 THINK

Read Revelation 22v20-21

How do you feel about Jesus coming back? Ask Him to get you excited about living with Him for ever. And ask Him to help you to serve Him until He comes.

 PRAY

Building up
Flick back through this issue of Table Talk to remind yourselves of some of the things you've read in God's Word, the Bible. Thank Him for the things He has been teaching you.

Extra Readings

WHY ARE THERE EXTRA READINGS?

Table Talk and **XTB** both come out every three months. The main Bible reading pages contain material for 65 days. That's enough to use them Monday to Friday for three months.

Many families find that their routine is different at weekends from during the week. Some find that regular Bible reading fits in well on school days, but not at weekends. Others encourage their children to read the Bible for themselves during the week, then explore the Bible together as a family at weekends, when there's more time to do the activities together.

The important thing is to help your children get into the habit of reading the Bible for themselves—and that they see that regular Bible reading is important for **you** as well.

If you **are** able to read the Bible with your children every day, that's great! The extra readings on the next page will augment the main **Table Talk** pages so that you have enough material to cover the full three months.

You could:

- Read **Table Talk** every day for 65 days, then use the extra readings for the rest of the third month.

- Read **Table Talk** on weekdays. Use the extra readings at weekends.

- Use any other combination that works for your family.

END TO END BIBLE TIMELINE

HISTORY = HIS STORY. These extra readings will whiz you through all the people and events on your **Bible Timeline**, from the very <u>beginning</u> to the very <u>end</u>.

These extra readings come from many different books in the Bible. They start with Genesis—the very first book in the Bible—and zoom all the way through to Revelation.

There are 26 Bible readings on the next three pages. Part of each verse has been printed for you—but with a word missing. Fill in the missing words as you read the verses. Then see if you can find them all in the wordsearch.

Note: Some are written backwards—or diagonally!!

A	P	I	C	K	E	D	E	N	E	V	A	E	H	B
M	N	X	T	B	K	I	N	G	R	A	N	D	L	E
A	M	G	A	P	E	V	E	R	Y	T	H	I	N	G
Z	O	I	E	B	I	B	L	E	H	E	R	E	S	I
E	S	D	B	L	E	S	S	E	D	E	A	T	H	N
D	E	E	P	O	H	E	A	R	T	U	K	N	O	N
L	S	O	B	E	D	A	M	E	N	A	N	D	P	I
A	S	N	A	G	S	R	U	L	E	B	O	C	R	N
U	H	O	L	Y	D	R	E	A	M	C	W	L	A	G
G	X	T	B	P	U	C	L	O	T	H	S	O	Y	X
H	E	M	I	T	J	O	S	H	U	A	O	U	E	T
H	O	L	Y	S	P	I	R	I	T	I	N	D	D	B

Extra Readings

1 ☐ **Read Genesis 1v1-5**

God made our world, our universe, and everything in them.

'In the **b** _ _ _ _ _ _ _
God created the heavens
and the earth.' (v1)

2 ☐ **Read Genesis 3v1-13**

God made the first family—Adam and Eve. But they broke God's laws. This is called sin.

'The woman took some of the fruit and
a _ _ it. She also gave some to her
husband, and he ate it.' (v6)

3 ☐ **Read Genesis 6v9-22**

The people of the world were so wicked that God decided to wash it clean with a flood. God saved the only good man—Noah—and his family.

'Noah did
e _ _ _ _ _ _ _ _ _ _
that God commanded.' (v22)

4 ☐ **Read Genesis 12v1-5**

God made three amazing promises to Abraham: 1—a huge family; 2—a land of their own; 3—someone from this family would be God's way of blessing the whole world.

'All the people on earth will be
b _ _ _ _ _ _ _ through you.' (v3)

5 ☐ **Read Genesis 21v1-7**

When Abraham was 100 years old, he had the son God had promised. His son was called Isaac, which means 'he laughs'.

'Sarah said, "God has brought me laughter. Everyone who hears about this will
l _ _ _ _ with me.' (v6)

6 ☐ **Read Genesis 25v19-26**

When Isaac grew up he became the father of twins—Esau (the hairy one!) and Jacob (the smoothie!).

'Isaac's wife could not have
children, so Isaac **p** _ _ _ _ _ _
to the LORD for her.' (v21)

7 ☐ **Read Genesis 37v1-11**

Jacob had twelve sons—but Joseph was his favourite.

'Joseph had a **d** _ _ _ _ _ . When he
told it to his brothers they hated him all the
more.' (v5)

8 ☐ **Read Exodus 3v1-10**

The story of Joseph ends with the Israelites living in Egypt. But after 400 years, the Egyptians made them into slaves! So God chose Moses to rescue them.

'I am sending you to the king of Egypt
(Pharaoh) to bring my people out of
E _ _ _ _ _ .' (v10)

9 ☐ **Read Joshua 4v19-24**

After 40 years wandering in the desert, Joshua led the Israelites into the promised land of Canaan.

' The Lord did this so that all the people of
the earth might **k** _ _ _ how great the
LORD's power is.' (v24)

10 ☐ **Read Judges 7v19-23**

Gideon was one of the Judges who rescued the Israelites from their enemies.

'They shouted, "A sword for the LORD and for
G _ _ _ _ _ _ ." ' (v20)

Extra Readings

11 ☐ **Read Ruth 2v11-12**

Ruth came from the country of Moab—but she married Boaz (an Israelite) and became the great-grandmother of King David!
'Ruth's son was called **O** _ _ _ . He was the father of Jesse, who was the father of David.' (v12)

12 ☐ **Read 1 Samuel 2v18-21**

God answered Hannah's prayer, and gave her a son—Samuel. So she gave Samuel back to God to serve Him.
'The boy **S** _ _ _ _ _ grew up serving the LORD.' (v21)

13 ☐ **Read 1 Samuel 10v17-25**

The Israelites demanded a king (even though <u>God</u> was their Real King!). Their first king was called Saul.
'The people shouted, "Long live the **k** _ _ _ !" ' (v24)

14 ☐ **Read 1 Samuel 16v1-13**

When Saul turned away from God, God chose David to be the next king of Israel. David's heart was full of love for God.
'People look at the outward appearance, but the LORD looks at the **h** _ _ _ _ .' (v7)

15 ☐ **Read 1 Kings 3v5-14**

David's son, Solomon, asked God for wisdom so that he could rule the Israelites well.
'Without wisdom it is impossible to **r** _ _ _ this great people of yours.' (v9)

16 ☐ **Read Daniel 6v16-23**

Daniel trusted and obeyed God—even when it meant being thrown to the lions!
'My God sent His **a** _ _ _ _ to shut the mouths of the lions.' (v22)

17 ☐ **Read Esther 4v12-16**

Esther was a Jewish girl who became queen of Persia. She risked her life to save the rest of the Jews from an evil plot.
'You may have been chosen queen for just such a **t** _ _ _ as this.' (v14)

18 ☐ **Read Nehemiah 2v1-6**

Like Esther, Nehemiah also risked the king's anger to help his fellow Jews (Israelites).
'I prayed to the God of **h** _ _ _ _ _ .' (v4)

19 ☐ **Read Luke 2v1-7**

Jesus was born in Bethlehem— the town David had been born in 1000 years earlier.
'Mary wrapped the baby in **c** _ _ _ _ _ and laid Him in a manger.' (v7)

20 ☐ **Read Matthew 3v13-17**

When Jesus was baptised by John the Baptist, God voice was heard. God called Jesus His loved Son.
'This is my **S** _ _ whom I love.' (v17)

This is my Son.

Extra Readings

21 ☐ **Read John 5v1-9**

Jesus did amazing miracles. He healed sick people, stopped a storm by speaking to it, and even brought dead people back to life!

'At once the man was cured. He

p _ _ _ _ _ up his mat and walked.' (v9)

22 ☐ **Read Matthew 7v24-29**

Jesus' teaching is hugely important. <u>Not</u> obeying His words is as disastrous as your house falling down!

'The crowds were **a** _ _ _ _ _ _ at His teaching.' (v28)

23 ☐ **Read Matthew 28v1-10**

When Jesus died on the cross it was <u>not</u> the end—because God brought Him back to life again!

'He is not **h** _ _ _ ; He has risen, just as He said He would.' (v6)

24 ☐ **Read Acts 1v9-11**

Jesus went up (ascended) into heaven. One day He will come back again.

'Jesus was taken up before their very eyes, and a **c** _ _ _ _ hid Him from their sight.' (v9)

25 ☐ **Read Acts 2v1-13**

When the first Christians were given the Holy Spirit, He helped them to tell others all about Jesus.

'They were all filled with the

H _ _ _ **S** _ _ _ _ _ _

and began to talk in other languages.' (v4)

26 ☐
Read Revelation 21v1-4

John saw a vision of heaven. One day, all followers of Jesus will live with Him in heaven.

'There will be no more **d** _ _ _ _ or sadness or crying or pain.' (v4)

WHAT NEXT?

We hope that **Table Talk** has helped you get into a regular habit of reading the Bible with your children. The twelve issues of Table Talk cover the main Bible books, characters and events.

Table Talk 1: The Book of Beginnings
(Genesis, Matthew, Acts)

Table Talk 2: Miracles and Dreams
(Genesis, Matthew, Acts)

Table Talk 3: Comings and Goings
(Exodus, Matthew, Acts)

Table Talk 4: Travels Unravelled
(Exodus, Matthew, Acts)

Table Talk 5: The Promise Keeper
(Numbers, Mark, Ephesians)

Table Talk 6: Footprints
(Joshua, Mark, Ephesians)

Table Talk 7: Heroes and Zeros
(Judges, Ruth, Mark)

Table Talk 8: The Real King
(1 Samuel, Mark, Psalms)

Table Talk 9: Way to Go
(2 Samuel, John)

Table Talk 10: Check It Out
(1 Kings, 2 Kings, John)

Table Talk 11: Write and Wrong
(2 Kings, Isaiah, Jeremiah, John)

Table Talk 12: End to End
(Daniel, Nehemiah, John, Revelation)

Available from your local Christian bookshop—or call us on **0845 225 0880** to order a copy.